The Flight of the Throstle

WBA in the early 1990's

By Simon Wright

Introduction

The 1990's remains a neglected period in West Bromwich Albion's recent history. With the exception of the Ardiles year, a whole decade is sidelined. Yet it was in this era that the Baggies slowly built foundations for our current lofty status.

Every season has moments worthy of recording for posterity, both on and off the pitch. Football is far more than passive entertainment, it's about people, family, places, history, social culture – it's a way of life.

The *Flight of the Throstle* aims to fill the early 1990's gap before precious emotional memories fail completely. As I've discovered, personal anecdotes are already hard to track down. It's a sobering thought for me that Albion supporters entering their mid-thirties (now the majority) were too young to remember the start of the 1990's. Thus detailed accounts of a period which featured low technology, high fences, terraces, smoking and 3pm kick-offs will be alien concepts.

"Flight" examines how Albion slipped into the (real) Third Division and escaped Phoenix-like only after two years of struggle. Along the way, some myths get busted and alfresco football and fan power are both relived, all leavened with numerous humourous anecdotes.

A quarter of a century ago - in a less sophisticated world - we had dreams, a hunger and a belief to drive us forward that one day we would overcome and aspire to bigger goals. In 2016, West Bromwich Albion are a big club again with worldwide appeal. And a glass ceiling. Simon

As it Was

The passing of time has added a faint rosy-hued tint to supporting Albion back in 1990, eroding the edge from the gritted-teeth fury and frustration from a period when the Millennium was a future IT calamity.

Let me describe going to the match for the benefit of younger generations. Note not the "*matchday experience*" – Jeremy's management speak was not heard around the Hawthorns until well into the following decade.

A popular myth did the rounds that watching Albion completely sober was not sensible. Fortunately, a range of highly convenient watering holes nearly ringed the ground to meet this need. The diminutive Woodman pub, nestling behind the Woodman corner terrace, was in vogue and crammed every game with people and smoke. On the other side of the stadium was the large but tatty Grade 2 listed Hawthorns Hotel, which had its own devotees. In Halfords Lane was the elderly but capacious Throstles Club, which boasted a first-class bowling green and a car park whose pock-marked surface resembled the moon. This was no laughing matter for night games. In the absence of TV football, supporters talked more and drank more – if they could get served. (Televised football in 1990 was a single live First Division match on a Sunday, plus highlights on Match of the Day. As the team of the decade, Liverpool were regularly featured)

Albion's commercial income in general was limited. The club sponsors were Sandwell Council, who gave WBA £250,000 to carry the name on the shirts. Supporters of other local clubs were highly unimpressed, and, of course, the concept of "football on the rates" quickly became a stick to beat councillors with. Even through rose-tinted spectacles, it was not easy to work out what return the Council received on their investment. As a public sector body, Sandwell Council were not in competition with anyone.

The unremarkable Albion programme was sold only inside the ground. This was due to real or perceived concerns about sellers' safety dating back to incidents ten years previously. Such lazy marketing meant the Hawthorns exterior was the sole domain of Grorty Dick fanzine, then a new publication still feeling its way, but already fulminating. This two-step arrangement confused visitors and irregular supporters for a full decade. *"Is that the programme?"* tested the patience of any fanzine seller. Also on sale in the streets was the Supporters Club publication "Fingerpost" though on its last legs. A succession of editors had tried and failed to be frank about the Baggies' shortcomings without upsetting either the Supporters Club Committee or WBA.

The club's twin interfaces with supporters - the Club Shop and ticket office - were inside the same door off Halfords Lane. They were modern, but woefully small for purpose. One infamous picture of the period revealed two big blokes completely filling the club shop simply by standing in it.

The Club Shop was routinely ridiculed for its small size and tiny range. As supporter Geoff Tustin put it *"Albion's cave, deep in the heart of the main stand, where with three people at the counter, it's impossible to see what's on offer. The amount of people who turn away at the sight of the queue is immeasurable."* Albion Secretary Gordon Bennett pointed out that club shop takings had trebled in its Halfords Lane location. Undoubtedly true, but the starting base must have been very low. The Club Shop manager admitted that *"we can't sell more than 50 of anything,"* while privately, the shop staff were as frustrated as the supporters. They were jammed shoulder-to-shoulder behind the counter, endlessly apologising for the absence of club shirts.

Meanwhile across the hall, was the Ticket Office. In these pre-internet days, buying a ticket meant travelling to the ground. Endless queuing for the occasional big game was both normal and predictable.

Indeed, there was very little consideration for supporter comfort. There were no traffic lights at the Halfords Lane/Brummie Road junction so fans ran across four lanes of traffic. No safety lanes for pedestrians along the Brummie Road, or any fencing along the pavement. Halfords Lane remained fully open at all times before the match. Most stewards didn't have radios – neither did many of the Police who were often unpaid Specials. Mobile phones were both bulky and rare. These were simpler times but any emergency was hard to resolve.

So simple that season ticket holders had a book of paper vouchers – one per game, to be handed to the generally glum turnstile operators. Those same season ticket holders had to pay rather more for their regular football fix. A Brummie Road annual ticket cost £85 – a 54% increase on the previous season, which prompted raucous complaints. By way of comparison, Man City charged £45 for standing season tickets with Leeds at £60. Cheapest on the door admission was a fiver, up markedly on the £4 from the previous season, and the same price would gain entry at Old Trafford. This really was cash on the door – tickets were rarely needed, home or away. To add financial context to the pricing, the UK average weekly wage was £320, unemployment was at a 12-year low, and the average house price in London was £82,000.

Once inside the Hawthorns, both the Brummie Road (popular) and the 'Smerrick' (unpopular) were terraces. Supporters happily stood up for the whole game, although bizarrely sat on the concrete steps before kick-off and at half time. If a supporter didn't like the person standing next to them, or objected to smoking, which was then legal, he or she moved away. Radical stuff! Cigarette smoke always lingered around the Hawthorns and the bigger the game, the heavier the clouds of smoke. The singers stood together at the centre back of the 14,000 capacity Brummie.

Next to the Brummie was the unroofed Woodman corner terrace, which backed onto the pub. This narrow enclosure had its own devotees, being traditionally the area for neutrals. Woodman regular Russell Cook explained *"We exist in limbo, trapped between the partisan fervour of the Brummie Road and the forlorn apathy of the Rainbow Stand, so understandably we display distinct characteristics of this interbreeding. Goals are celebrated with clenched fists, ritual leaping about, and a celebratory Rothmans King Size, while defeat is borne in grim faced silence."* At the back of the Woodman was the fine old wooden scoreboard, where large printed numbers to indicate the score were inserted next to a letter. A key in the programme listed the bigger matches of the day, with a letter against each one. Match A was Arsenal v Sheffield United, B Coventry v Norwich and so on. The only alternative for keeping up to date with other games was "tranny man" – the much-ridiculed but often exploited supporter with a small radio pressed to their ear.

Next to the Woodman was the old Rainbow Stand, with its elderly wooden seats, and a steep flight of uncovered stairs at the back. These stairs could be treacherous during icy weather. Sitting down was considered elitist during this era – the preserve of wealthy people, or the elderly. The lower set of seats – known as the Paddock – were closed to ensure that the box holders' views were unimpeded. Keeping the box holders humming was considered more important than the club's public image. Blocks of empty seats looked so poor on the few occasions that TV crews visited The Hawthorns. Behind the Rainbow Stand was a big car park, and the boarded-up ruin of another capacious Throstles Club.

Behind the opposite goal was the "Smerrick" then a large covered terrace, split by high fencing to accommodate away supporters. Like the Brummie, each concrete step in the "Smerrick" was low meaning a hard time for short supporters. But in practice, given our meagre attendances, size rarely mattered. Although an ideal position to exchange "pleasantries" with the visitors, the "Smerrick" was unfashionable and thinly populated. It did enjoy a reputation for being alternative and "edgy."

The most modern part of the stadium was the Halfords Lane stand, which, even then, was thought to be occupied by elderly men bearing travel rugs and thermos flasks. In this era, facilities were limited so bringing your own refreshments was a sound idea. The refreshment hut served brown liquid in lidless plastic cups which was both tea and coffee. Also, the regular absence of toilet tissue in Halfords Lane was an occupational hazard, and hot water was something that only Albion managers got into. Many visitors learnt the hard way that not every seat were actually attached to its toilet. Yet Halfords Lane facilities were an improvement on the rest of the Hawthorns. The Birmingham Road toilets were notorious for overflowing and were the home of several strange organic bodies, some previously unknown to science. Frankly, they were quite appalling even by the laidback standards of the time. Directors were regularly invited to look into them but without any noticeable improvement.

In this era, match goers were considered guilty until proven innocent, so both terraces had ten foot high perimeter fences. They were erected a decade earlier and always resented. Fencing was normal in the Football League but with the horror of Hillsborough still so fresh, their days were numbered. As an interim measure, there was great emphasis laid upon numerous access gates, manned by stewards. This was a comfort, for in recent years, travelling Albion supporters endured several small-scale incidents which avoided squashing injuries more by luck than judgement.

There were rarely fences in front of seated areas, due to the curious logic that people initially sitting down couldn't possibly have any violent intent. This logic was lampooned regularly with the chant "*seats are evil...*"

The perception of violence was, as ever, significantly stronger than the reality. During the period, the Police acted first and sometimes asked questions later, comfortable that as football supporters were second class citizens they could get away with anything. Non-football lovers had a fixed image that every match every week resembled a war zone. Offer a friend a free ticket for (say) a midweek fixture against Barnsley, and their first question would inevitably be: "*what about the violence?*" Many people stayed away, including one Jeremy Peace *"I didn't go for about ten years because of the violence."* Police – supporter relations was simply dreadful and a comment doing the rounds at the time was "*at the Hawthorns, away supporters are automatically ejected.*"

Not that we had it any easier "on the road." Supporters travelling by coach, even those officially organised, were treated with suspicion. Police regularly boarded to give "do's and don'ts" lectures. Some officers tried for empathy, but others merely peddled the boorish party line. Hold-ups, petty delays and unwanted Police escorts were normal. So too were arrests. There was a perception that more arrests meant justification of their overtime payments. Despite the fences, aggressive attitudes from Police, stewards and some supporters, the regulars knew there were very few violent incidents at Baggies matches. There were exceptions and memories remained raw of Everton fan Rob McMurray being blinded in one eye after being attacked near the Hawthorns in 1989. I organised a ground collection and a benefit match raised £3,000 for Rob (then the equivalent of 35 season tickets) but the damage couldn't be fully undone. Rob used the money as a mortgage deposit but several years passed before he felt able to return to active football-watching.

A series of violent incidents elsewhere typically produced an ill- thought out knee-jerk reaction from the Government. Thatcher's Conservatives planned to introduce ID cards for all supporters. This threat had only just been fought off with some residual pride in that West Bromwich Albion supporters had been the first to mobilise. The local Football Supporters Association worked together with the fanzine to persuade 5,000 people to sign a petition prior to a Crystal Palace match in the late 1980's. This event was even mentioned on the Radio 2 Headlines (the equivalent of the modern Radio 5) before the football results. So many Albion supporters asked for blank petition forms for their friends and workmates to sign, that the final number exceeded 10,000 – almost equivalent to an average gate. Like flying pickets, determined Albionites went on to fill up petition boards at Coventry, Old Trafford and the League Cup Final at Wembley. It was an impressive show of fan power solidarity.

With average attendances only filling a third of the ground, individual voices or groups could be heard easily. Smaller gates made for different dynamics. There were, of course, plus points around ease of entry, getting to and from the Hawthorns, car parking, and access to your favourite spot. More importantly, there was a village feel among the regulars. Everyone knew everyone else if by face if not by name. We were a put-upon unappreciated elite, which engendered a collective sense of pride and unity for sticking with the club in difficult times. Humour, often black, was sought and shared diligently. Most often, we moaned a lot. There was so much to complain about. Four years absence from the top flight, the appalling Saunders era, poor players, the state of the club finances, and the false dawn under Talbot were all rich sources of grievance.

Fortunately, our neighbours also had little to shout about. Aston Villa resided in the top flight, but had quickly found themselves at the wrong end of the table. The Tatters ('Dingles' came much later) were a nuisance to us in the Second Division. Such a modest status was beyond moribund Birmingham City, who struggled vainly to get out of the Third Division while Walsall were just Walsall, no threat to anyone.

The 1990's opens

As the new decade began, Brian Talbot's men were in a worrying 19th position in the Second Division (the second tier of English football) and having one of their worst League seasons at home since the war.

The first visitors of the new decade were Brighton. Primarily because of their name-stealing tactics, the Sussex mob has never been taken seriously, either on the pitch or off it. "Imitation Albion," as they were regularly lampooned by Baggies regulars, were easily beaten 3-0.   The win was savoured by the massed ranks of -err... 9,400. There were to be no more home League victories for three months. The crowd shrunk during the game as several visitors were escorted out for "arguing." Regular ejections were all too common in the away end.

Stuart Naylor was Albion's regular 'keeper, the last remnant of the infamous 1985-86 relegation squad. "Bruiser" or *"Come off your line, Naylor"* was a survivor who always found a way back after being dropped. He was the Baggies fourth different keeper since August.

In front of him were the first choice pairing of Stacey North and Chris "Huggy" Whyte. Whyte was rescued from America, his place of refuge after he'd been forced to leave Arsenal. His height and calm assurance made him one of the stars of the team. His long throw-ins were something to behold. The other main man was Don Goodman, famed for his pace, goals, falling over and rampant hair.

There were numerous local players in the squad. Shakespeare, Foster, Burgess, Dobbins, Bradley, Thomas and Hackett were all born within 15 miles of the Hawthorns. The entire squad were British-born with a total cost of £1.25 million. They played in a 4-4-2 formation just like everyone else. Was there any other way? The few teams who went with

5-3-2 were roundly criticised for their boring, negative tactics. The Baggies problem was one of consistency, both in results and team composition. 31 players turned out during 1989-90, including a token appearance from assistant manager Sam Allardyce, in an embarrassing 5-1 home defeat by Newcastle late in the season. The big Dudley-born defender was never the same again and, to this day, rarely misses a chance to have a dig at the Baggies.

 On their day, which usually came in cup matches, West Bromwich Albion could defend stoutly and attack with pace. They'd beaten Newcastle on their own pitch in the League Cup against the odds. The week after beating Brighton in the League, WBA comfortably defeated First Division Wimbledon in the Cup. Their reward was another top flight side at home – Charlton.

Despite a miserable recent record, Albion supporters still believed in the magic of the Cup, and the turn-out for the Londoners was impressive. Too impressive for the football club who were badly caught out. The attendance of 18,000 was a third larger than the average, but way lower than the ground capacity. Supporters queuing in heavy rain were unamused. People forced into the open Woodman terrace because the rest of the stadium was allegedly full, were mad as hornets. *"It was more than a torrential downpour – for the ninety minutes of that game, I felt the full weight of the Albion board and backroom staff pissing down on me – from a very great height"* lamented Adrian Goldberg, then co-editor of the seminal Off the Ball fanzine. Bizarrely, some Albion supporters were turned away altogether. Not everyone had the imagination of musician Kevin Sect who talked his way through two rows of suspicious Police into the covered away end, which, predictably, was half-empty.

The deluge continued as the Baggies beat Charlton who "didn't fancy it" on a bog of a pitch. Historian Steve Carr couldn't *"ever recall seeing our pitch in such a state. The midfield resembled a Somme battlefield, and either end was a paddy field."* Albion won through a freak Tony Ford goal. The ball was rolling towards the post until water power deflected it crucially over the line. Charlton missed a penalty, and hit both posts in the closing minutes. The whole sodden affair was featured in a very rare appearance on Match of the Day.

Also this month, Lord Justice Taylor published his final report on the Hillsborough disaster. Crucially, he didn't support ID cards, and this, combined with the imminent end of the reign of Margaret Thatcher, finally killed the concept. Taylor's solution to make all top clubs go all-seater would change our game markedly.

The FA Cup Fifth Round draw paired the Baggies with the Old Enemy – Villa, at the Hawthorns. The match was all-ticket, but with the capacity artificially limited to 26,000 – some two thousand lower than the gate for the derby against Wolverhampton. Once again, the football club did their best to annoy or confuse.

Prices were raised. No postal applications were allowed. Season ticket holders had the same priority as Members – a category which required no more commitment than submitting two passport photographs - and holders of vouchers given out at the previous League game. There was only one option- turn up on a freezing Sunday morning and queue, or find a mug to do it for you. No toilets, no cover or any refreshments (no McDonalds then) were provided.

The queue was spectacular. From the under-siege ticket office, it stretched out of the door, up Halfords Lane, the full width of the Brummie, then on past the Woodman, Concentric Engineering and even Apollo 2000. At its peak, tail-end Charlies were lining up in Middlemore Road. A waiting time of 3 hours was common, and confusion over how many tickets were left created more unrest.

After such a wretched experience, how sad that in the big match Albion rarely worried Villa. Their hopes were badly damaged by losing the in-form Gary Robson after just four minutes, and the damaged pitch bought the Baggies down to Villa's level. Goals from Mountfield (first half) and Daley (last minute) ended any ambition of further progress. Beating Villa was to remain an unfulfilled dream until 2011. Bizarrely, the Albion News that day included pen pictures of the home team. Just to make matters worse, there was much squabbling in the Rainbow as lots of Villains had bought tickets in the home end.

Once out of the Cup, the rest of the season seemed rather flat and frustrating. The team were back to inconsistent performances and results.

One notable exception was a trip to the all-conquering Leeds United in February. The Whites were on the way to promotion and boasted the startling aggressive midfield of Gordon Strachan, Vinny Jones, Chris Kamara and David Batty. There was just one small area of uncovered terrace in the whole ground so naturally that was for us. After 45 minutes of heavy rain and United dominance, resignation was universal. We mournfully chorused "Singing in the Rain" and pointedly refused to join in Leeds' Mexican wave.

At half time, there was a dash for the only cover – the Gents toilet. Those who wished to use the facilities for their normal purpose had to fight their way through smokers, pie eaters and coffee drinkers all seeking shelter. Around 150 supporters crammed in. For once, there was a happy ending – United became complacent after going two up. Leeds-born Goodman and then Kevin Bartlett both sprung their frequently used offside trap to bring back an unexpected and jolly welcome point. Ah yes, Kevin Bartlett. He was a very, very fast striker, purchased from Cardiff, who didn't really have much else to offer. His legacy is a chant "*Oh Kevin B. from*

Cardiff C, Oh Kevin B. from Cardiff C. He's got a head like a Malteser. Oh Kevin from Cardiff C."

This was an alternative and lesser-known version of a quirky Albion classic. Another of the not-quite-decent strikers during this period was John Thomas, genuinely Black Country born and Albion was always his team. He was a down-to-earth character who ran a stall in Wednesbury Market. *"Oh Johnny T from Wednesbury, Oh Johnny T from Wednesbury. He's got a stall on the market. Oh Johnny T from Wednesbury."* This irresistible number was first aired at a midweek game at Bournemouth and rapidly caught on, courtesy of its author, long-time fan Fabrize "Fab" Tracanna. John Thomas now owns a sizable sportswear business in Bolton.

Having already lost to the Tatters at home, another defeat in the return fixture at the Custard Bowl in March was beyond the pale. Thoughts of the derby started with the usual ticket sales confusion. The press and the Albion News stated tickets were sold out (they hadn't) while during the same home match, announcements were made about when to queue for tickets. That year, only the huge terraced South Bank was open at Molineux. A 20-yard buffer zone ensured that the rabid, slavering home hordes kept their distance. Adrian Foster made his most positive contribution to club history by scoring first, but after that, Albion defended badly and lost 2-1. Just to rub it in, there was no Police escort to the station or any football special running, just when they were needed most. Relegation remained a threat until the 45th League match – a trip to Barnsley. Then as now, Albion couldn't win in the land of the flat cap, whippet and coal mine. Fortunately, a draw would do and they would be urged on by a huge support. The first ever Baggies Beach Party at Hull the previous year was such a massive success that everyone was up for a repeat. The Travellers Arms pub in Birdwell near Barnsley built a football-friendly reputation, rare in this era. Over 100 Albion supporters packed in that morning, enjoying free food laid on by mine host Dick, before heading for Oakwell. Here, over 3,500 of the Black Country's finest, plus inflatables and balloons, paid £3.50 to stand on a big, open terrace. Around 60% wore beachwear or fancy dress but all were in good heart, a mood heightened by an upbeat PA message *"Welcome to the supporters from West Bromwich Albion – you're the most colourful supporters we've seen this season."* There were many pictures taken of the joyful mob but one image summed up the day – an Albion supporter in lurid shorts and flat cap, cheerfully waving an inflatable woman. The strong wind was to whisk away most of the balloons. They landed in their hundreds on a bowling green behind the away end. With Francis Drake stoicism, a group of old gentlemen continued to play bowls, ignoring the inflatables descending like confetti all around them.

Albion showed the same grit on their pitch, holding out against a strong Barnsley team while nicking two goals on the break. A late Tykes equaliser prevented a win but with relegation rivals Bournemouth losing, a draw was good news all round. The referee's final whistle prompted a good-natured pitch invasion from Barnsley supporters. Once they had cleared, firstly Gary Robson, and then the manager came out to show his appreciation followed by, after much urging, by the rest of the team. There was more positive feedback from Barnsley, with another message *"Thanks to everyone from West Brom for dressing up. You've added a lot of colour to Barnsley and you're a credit to the game. We'll see you next season in Division Two."*

 Staying up in such a positive, celebratory atmosphere reinforced the appeal of the end of season theme. It also confirmed that if we wanted entertainment, we had to create their own. The Supporters Club football team, the Strollers certainly did. Their Barnsley counterparts invited them to be guests at the Barnsley Supporters Club Player of the Year night for what turned out to be a long night of beer and lusty singing. Other fans headed back to the Travellers Arms for more Magnet, plus pizza and chips. Following a pit stop at another pub on the way home, well-known Albion carouser Colin Wood from South Wales enjoyed himself so much that he refused to leave so he was left behind. By Sunday afternoon, his journey back to the land of the Raincloud had only got as far as Great Barr, and he was sporting completely different clothes. Such minor difficulties rarely worried Colin... In the final home game against his old team Ipswich, manager Brian Talbot couldn't resist putting his boots on one more time. It didn't help. In a very downbeat final match, Albion lost 3-1. Not what we'd hoped for, and not even a particularly lengthy chorus of *"We hate Villa"* could sustain spirits for long. Many of the small crowd made for the exits before the end, grumbling loudly. Another home defeat (there were only six wins at the Hawthorns all season) felt like a bad future omen.

1990 91 – That Sinking Feeling

There were two pieces of good news during the summer. The Rainbow paddock was re-opened. The seats, low on the touchline and a sun trap during the warmer months, had a band of devotees, including the highly vocal "Chocolate Fudge-Cake Eaters" (best not to ask).The linesman was always fair game for wind-ups in their eyes.

The other development saw the hateful perimeter fencing lowered at either end of the stadium. The Taylor report forced expensive safety expenditure on clubs who retained full-height fences. With all-seater grounds on the way, these viewing barriers were doomed. The lowering of the barriers were a tentative first step towards treating supporters with more respect.

"It's going to be a hard season" admitted Brian Talbot in an unguarded moment before hastily backtracking. Supporters knew he had it right the first time. It was going to be a very hard season. The first indicator came was a quite shocking 5-0 friendly defeat at Swansea. It wasn't so easy to dismiss the non-competitive 90 minutes as being unimportant, because Goodman was sent off. Our only goal scorer now had a three game ban. The dismissal was an omen as Goodman was to miss most of the season, an absence which impacted painfully on Albion's destiny.

The Welsh thrashing underlined that Albion were light without Whyte. The classy defender had transferred to Leeds for a tribunal-decided £450,000, having refused a new contract. He was reputedly offered £65,000 a year at Elland Road, then an extraordinary sum. Silly mistakes in his final season, mainly his tendency to give away needless free kicks, eroded the popularity of the often-enigmatic stopper so his departure met with dry eyes, but he was not easily replaced. Whyte won a League Championship medal two years later.

Replacements – what replacements? Footballing gypsy Barry Siddall arrived as reserve goalkeeper on cheap non-contract terms. His only appearance was to be in the aforementioned pre-season thrashing in the Land of the Heavy Rain. The solitary monetary signing was big central defender Gary Strodder from West Ham. Although his Route One style contrasted with Whyte's sophistication, Strod's up-and-at-'em-damn-hard technique would eventually make him a favourite. The new season kicked off at Pompey. August in the sunshine was definitely the best time for open terracing. I drove my little Fiat Uno even though a weak hatchback lock repeatedly allowed the hatch door to rise by itself. Several times the hatch opened on the motorway, followed by a cacophony of horns from other drivers, who imagined I wanted my tailgate flapping in the breeze. Fortunately, the football improved my mood.

Backed by 2,000 noisy supporters, the Baggies put on a decent showing, notably neat interplay between strikers Goodman and Bannister. Ford's early diving header gave us the lead, which Pompey levelled in the second half. There was no more scoring, despite an astonishing 11 minutes of added-on time. An away draw was a decent result for a club who hadn't won on the opening day since the 1970's.

A mixed bag of results followed, including an exit from the League Cup. The highlight was a 3-1 win at the Manor Ground, Oxford, one of the many old-style grounds no longer with us.

The 'Manor' was an ugly squatter within a highly affluent Oxford suburb. Each stand was constructed piecemeal without any regard to its neighbours and resembled a showroom for a football stand wholesaler.

Away supporters had Hobson's choice of either overpriced seats in a low stand, or a crazily shaped, small-stepped open terrace. The terrace was previously fronted by a fence of concentration camp proportions. Like Albion, Oxford had had to reduce the height of the fence to a level where some of the pitch was actually visible.

Access to terrace or seats was along the same narrow, ill-lit alleyway, separating the ground from the Sir John Radcliffe hospital. Follow that alleyway away from the ground past numerous splendid back gardens, and eventually it ended in a small Oxfordshire village, complete with two delightful pubs. It was only years later when these delights became widely known ... and then the U's moved.

After a stimulating 2-1 home victory over Bristol City, Albion maintained their unbeaten run with a draw at Hull. There was a cameo appearance here from gangling Ugo Ehiogu, cheered on by the 2,000 visitors from the Midlands who made up one third of the gate. Ugo already enjoyed cult status without actually making a full League appearance but he was never to get any closer to an Albion career.

Bottom of the table Hull had hit hard times. Rambling old Boothferry Park was sad and rundown, unpainted and rusty. The large visitors terrace was rudely cut in half by a new supermarket. It looked awful, but City weren't in any position to refuse the cash. In general, Second Division grounds were a varied bunch, although Prince Charles wasn't likely to enthuse over their architectural merits. Take Millwall (please do). The 90/91 visit was among the more unpleasant ones to Cold Blow Lane. Comparatively, anyway – no trip there was ever fun-filled. The memory of one of our coaches being stoned and boarded in the early 1980's wasn't easily forgotten.

The whole rubble-strewn area with its barbed wire and dark tunnels was incredibly dispiriting. Think of Small Heath before it was gentrified and throw in dollops of menace to get close to that grim dock neighbourhood. Visitors simply weren't welcome and few wanted to take the risk anyway.

Albion supporters queued for up to 25 minutes at a single turnstile to move into the visitors' cage. The next challenge was to find the spot which would give the best view of the action. For starters, a full height floodlight pylon, complete with its own perimeter fencing, squatted in the middle of the away section. So standing behind that was hardly realistic. To go to the front would mean peering through the cage bars and potentially getting wet (the low roof only covered the back half of the terrace). Halfway back then? Yep, other than to see anything along the left touchline needed a flexing of the knees, and a crane of the neck. As ever, supporters can put up with a lot if their team performs but the Lions' Teddy Sherringham scored twice in the first 8 minutes and the home side cantered to a 4-1 win. Who'd be an Albion supporter? The Baggies were missing out on crucial points, even when they managed a five match unbeaten run, for the lack of a regular goal scorer. Such missed opportunities would later return to haunt us. For instance, the gallant 700 who travelled to the far North-East were frustrated that Talbot's men had no more ambition than one point against an injury-wrecked Newcastle. The unluckiest group of all travelled on a Hawthorns Away Travel Section (HATS) coach whose driver bizarrely drove them to Hull, rather than Newcastle. Having been told his fortune, he finally got his passengers to St James for the second half – just in time for United's equaliser. Travelling away was more of a hit and miss affair in this decade, but this was spectacularly bad.

The Baggies needed an on-pitch leader to replace the manager so they signed former Spurs and England hard man Graham Roberts. Not everyone was impressed. Veteran fan Neil Reynolds gave away his season ticket. *"I never watched an Albion game while Roberts was playing for the club. One has to have certain standards and live by them, in all aspects of life. Roberts wasn't a footballer, he was a thug. If my team had to depend on players like that, it was no longer my team. I renewed the season ticket and started going again as soon as Roberts went. It would be the same now; if Albion suddenly turned into Stoke and played like them every week, they'd do it without me watching."* With hindsight, Neil made a wise decision.

On his Hawthorns debut against Blackburn Rovers, Roberts gave his youthful opponent a fearful whack after just two minutes play. Striker Lenny Johnrose spent the rest of the match keeping his distance, and Albion went on to win comfortably. Talk to professional footballers when off-duty and they'll just shrug off such tactics as being part of the game. But it's not part of the Beautiful Game for fans.

There wasn't much evidence of the beautiful game at the Hawthorns. Attendances shrunk to below 8,000. Results were poor, atmosphere poor, and understanding with the Police was also poor which all contributed to a self-perpetuating negative circle. The trip to table-topping West Ham encapsulated all the season's frustrations in one afternoon. The Albion support couldn't see the action thanks to a massive fence, not that there was much to see other than continuous one-way traffic towards their own goal. Possibly even worse, they were treated like cattle, penned in after the final whistle and then slow-marched to the tube station. West Ham supporters were prevented from using the tube until the visitors had gone and so took out their frustrations on the Black Country fans. It was as though nobody was allowed to enjoy themselves any more at a match.

During this period, Albion regularly conceded goals in the last ten minutes, most notably against the Tatters of Wolverhampton in the last game of the year. The home side had played well throughout, but when Naylor dropped a tame Dennison free kick, Hindmarch dived in. The glee from the "dark side" was too painful to stomach. Hindmarch received votes for 'Player of the Season' in the Wolves fanzine 'A Load of Bull' several years later on the strength of that goal – even after he'd left the club.

In fairness to WBA's No. 1, he'd hobbled through three games with a groin strain, with defenders taking his goal kicks. It said something about Naylor's qualities, or those of his latest deputy Mel Rees, that the situation continued for so long. But his painful groin, and presumably his restricted sex life, didn't protect Stuart from raucous supporter criticism. 'Bruiser' Naylor sounded calm, but probably wasn't. *"Everyone at the club seems to have been criticised this season. Now it's my turn."* The mood around the club was generally glum, and any player was seen as fair game for criticism.

The FA Cup always provided hope, a welcome diversion from League action. Albion needed some hope. But what they got was Woking. Only two Non-League sides left in the competition, and our ailing team copped for one of them. The fear started right then after the draw, a full month before the match. Exeter-based supporter Julian Rowe summed up concerns. *"A nightmare ever since the draw was made."*

 Years later, Darren Bradley admitted that *"we were in a bad way, and none of us were confident going into the tie."* Woking were confident of victory, despite their Isthmian Premier League status (one level below the Conference), having been just promoted to that level. They were used to winning, with 72 goals scored before Christmas, although Buzaglo only had 9 of those. Woking had belief, Albion didn't. It was with dread that I set out for the Hawthorns that Saturday. Prior to Woking, the Baggies had only won once in nine matches, and Goodman was a long term injury victim. Down on their uppers they may be, but West Bromwich Albion remained a proud old club, albeit one uncertain about non-professional players. They'd only played one other Non-League side since the war. The vultures were gathering to see the old king dethroned. Woking supporters were everywhere – some 5,000 of them taking over half the Smethwick End and the Rainbow Stand. The Press box was packed, and even the BBC smelt blood.

Unlike Woking, Albion lacked pace. Talbot paired Strodder with Graham Roberts at the back, and a less mobile pair it is hard to imagine. Behind them, goalkeeper Mel Rees made his debut. The whole side were just too nice (Roberts excepted), too lightweight and ideal for a small club wanting to make history. But the outcome could have been so different.

The first half was cagey, with both supporters and players nervous. Woking's Buzalgo was physically sick in the dressing room before kick-off. Close to the half-hour mark, "Westie" leapt high at the far post to reach Shakespeare's corner and the Baggies were one up. The relief was immense. It was as though the 10,000 strong faithful could now all breathe out at once. Colin West celebrated with the leaping Smethwick crew. Minutes later, Strodder could have doubled the lead. If his header had found the net – might history have been different?

At half-time, the Woking manager, Geoff Chapple, again reminded his players that Albion's defence was slow and easily turned. He highlighted the Baggies had managed to drop points from a winning position 9 times that season and even though the home players knew that their Woking counterparts had said *"we're going to thrash these"* and still they didn't react.

Play resumed, together with the nail-chewing. On the hour mark, Woking's Derek Brown's neat through ball set up Buzaglo to burst clear and equalise. The game and the mood changed immediately. It was all too damn easy, and the natives were restless.

Within six minutes, the Non-Leaguers were ahead as Buzaglo himself described. *"It came from a long clearance by our keeper Tim Read. Derek Brown flicked it on and the West Brom defenders Strodder and Roberts were a bit square. The ball looped over the top of them and I just ran past and scored."* Buzaglo was being modest. He tore between the defenders as though they were invisible, and somehow, squeezed the ball past the onrushing Rees.

There was just no way back for this limp Albion team. We supporters became increasingly wide-eyed and desperate. At one stage the ball went out of play in front of the Rainbow Stand. Fan Bob Lawley and his mate ran onto the pitch from the Rainbow Stand, His mate threw his scarf down, and stamped on it, in front of a very bemused Tony Ford. The stewards who escorted them away admitted later that given a free choice, they'd have left the fans on the pitch.

There was venom behind the choruses of *"Talbot Out"* and *"there's only one Bryan Robson"* from the fraught masses. Despite the strong cross-winds, it was the part-timers who had complete mastery of the football. They added a third ten minutes from time. Buzalgo polished off a seven-man move to complete his hat-trick. It is hard to imagine more polarised moods. Woking's massive virgin support was bouncing on the Smethwick terraces, whereas the rest of the ground was in dark, mutinous mood. More Black Country folk ran onto the pitch, but were quickly ushered away. With heavy symbolism, a black bin bag was thrown towards the pitch.

Woking scored again and the mood became even blacker, if possible. The Non Leaguers had only 6 shots in 90 minutes, but four of them ended up in Albion's net. Bradley's injury time goal was no consolation, indeed it was roundly booed by his own supporters, who had completely lost all rationality. Tears were shed and the language was industrial.

Come the end of this sad affair, there was a tidal-wave pitch invasion from the Brummie. It overwhelmed the thin line of Police. Some fans stopped to tell the Albion players exactly what they thought of them, particularly new Captain Graham Roberts, but the majority headed towards the away end. Buzalgo, being chaired by Woking people near the corner flag, must have feared the worst. To his own amazement and embarrassment, he was chaired round the ground by Albion fans. It was partly ironic celebration and partly a protest. *"Sign him up..."*

Brummie Road regular Steve Carr had his own memories: *"Woking were worthy winners, and their players went over to the Smethwick Corner to celebrate with their supporters. It was at this stage that a pitch invasion followed, and for a while the Woking players must have feared that they were in for a good kicking as an angry-looking Albion mob descended upon them. Whatever fears they had were groundless, however, as the Woking players were mobbed in a way that we would only expect our own to be, and many of them were lifted onto broad Black Country shoulders, and carried back to the Brummie Road End to receive a standing ovation from the many thousands who'd stayed behind. We realised that we'd witnessed a game that will remain a big part of Albion folklore. I joined in with the applause, stunned at what had happened, but utterly proud to be a Baggie that day in view of the way my fellow Baggies had acclaimed our conquerors. I can't imagine that Wolves fans would have acted in quite the same way!"*

Ian Hall, in his first season of Albion watching, was astonished to witness the swapping of shirts and scarves between fans. When Woking supporters were applauded as they left the ground, he quite forgot about the ineptness of the team's performance.

Veteran supporter Steve Sant focussed on the anger. "With the exception of the miners' strike and the poll tax protests, *I have seldom seen so many people so bloody angry. Everything you need to know about Baggies fans was encapsulated in the half hour which elapsed between 4.45 and*

5.15. *Disgusted, boiling with rage, cold and miserable, we stood on the half empty terraces desperate to let the club know exactly what we thought of it but few moved until the Woking players had been roundly applauded for their efforts.*" Pre-war Albion watcher and local radio "Terrace Talker" Terry Wills needed an outlet and quickly. *"Although Radio WM didn't require my services, I immediately hurried round to the press box and bluffed my way in. Fortunately the presenter Ian Winter knew good radio when he saw it and put me on. For the first time ever, I went for the jugular and verbally lashed Brian Talbot and his team. Ian's final question to me was "What's the way forward? "Talbot out and the sooner the better" was my fierce response.*

The protest outside the Directors entrance in Halfords Lane after the match was long and loud. Passing supporters were aggressively canvassed by angry protesters to join in.

Somebody Had To Be Blamed and both Brian Talbot and the entire Board were jointly held as scapegoats. *"Bring back our Albion to us"* was the mildest chant and *"Talbot must Go"* the most popular refrain.

As Don Goodman said *"we were humiliated, embarrassed. A part-time side trounced us and, even though I wasn't playing because of a calf strain, it didn't make the weekend pass any easier. I was in a foul mood and never forgot the experience."* Bernie McNally agreed: *"It was one of my embarrassing games ever. The players let the club down."* Chairman John Silk admitted: *"it was the blackest day in the history of West Bromwich Albion."*

Ian "Patch" Partridge was a scrapbook fanatic. Every match report was seized upon and carefully cut out and pasted onto a page. Post Woking he grabbed his entire scrapbook collection and threw them on a bonfire.

The BBC wanted a talking head for "human interest" so I did the honours for both Radio 2 and TV. The latter ended up as a curious downbeat tailpiece of the first Albion History video. I've never been allowed to forget the Kevin Keegan perm and my yellow and red anorak.

Two days after the premature Cup exit, Brian Talbot was sacked (coincidentally Villa manager John Ward also got the bullet on the same day). Talbot had been on the slippery slope for months. The obvious difficulty was *"who next?"* As Yorkshire-based Baggie Lars Neale suggested *"my fear is that the board panicked when faced with the scenes after the Woking game without having a notion of who to replace him with."* The problem for the Board and supporters alike was that there was no obvious successor.

Stuart Pearson became caretaker. He was quick to point out he'd previously told Talbot that long ball wouldn't work. Setting his cap at the job permanently, Pancho immediately introduced passing football, a new 3-5-2 formation, and had the players training both morning and afternoon.

Desperate supporters got behind him at once. The acting manager's' biggest problems were a lengthy injury list, and a morale-shattered squad. Still the players rallied, and in the next six games, Pearson's charges won two, drew one and lost three. This modest record left room for argument either way regarding his suitability. His highlight was a slick 3-0 victory at Ewood Park as a fine display of passing football ripped Rovers wide open. The away-day experience was heightened by mass handouts of Fishermens Friends lozenges and a pre-match drink in the Fernhurst. In 1991, being encouraged to enter an away-fan friendly pub by the local rozzers was a revelation.

However, there was a common perception that Pearson allowed his players the choice to train or not as they wished. Certainly, the caretaker himself was reluctant to accept any degree of separation from the players. *"I want the players to call me Pancho, buy me a pint and share a round of golf with* me." His incautious remark that Albion *"would need ten years to put together a promotion team"* brought forward predictable knee-jerk criticism. History would prove his prediction was only two years out.

At this delicate time, West Bromwich Albion needed all the friends they could get. So banning umbrellas on the Woodman Corner because they were an "offensive weapon" was particularly crass. The handful of regulars who continued to use the only section of uncovered terrace at the Hawthorns sighed deeply. As if they didn't have enough reason to be very angry already....

Almost two months elapsed without a permanent manager. Journalist Jeff Prestridge was among those peeved over the delay. *"The Board's huffing and puffing over finding a replacement – Major Cox, Brainy Sexton, Waffly Warnock or Bombastic Bobby – was the killer blow."* The media were convinced that Alan Buckley would get the job. Then they insisted it was Mel Machin and then Arthur Cox.... Meanwhile Graham Roberts was telling everyone that he wanted the job himself, promising to bring in his mate Glenn Hoddle to assist. The saga dragged painfully on and on, further lowering spirits among supporters.

Although doubt remained whether Stuart Pearson was "our man", there was unanimous agreement that we did not want long-ball hoofer Bobby Gould of Wimbledon infamy in charge. Rumours persisted as early as the previous October that Gould would move in at WBA.

At Ipswich, the message was clear *"We don't want your Bobby Gould".* The message was repeated more loudly at Blackburn, and then, with desperate vehemence, at home to Notts County. Three days later, John Silk and his merry men appointed Bobby Gould. *"We look forward to a long and successful period with him in charge"* ventured the Albion News, ever hopefully.

Bobby Gould was a former Albion player. Not a popular one as during his short spell in the early 1970's, he was considered a 'nark' for manager Don Howe. His team-mates recalled that he'd managed to annoy all of them on his first day of training. Supporters with long memories remember howling their annoyance after Gould missed a sitter against Newcastle, and receiving a two-fingered salute in response. The King, Jeff Astle, dismissed him *"as just a runner with no talent"* and *"a terrible player who couldn't trap a bag of cement."*

Gould's forte was scoring goals, a feat which will always sustain a career though curiously clubs only seemed to have success after they'd shipped him out. He departed from Arsenal just before their double-winning season, Wolves prior to their run to the UEFA Cup Final, and ditto West Ham in the Cup Winners' Cup. It was far from unknown for officials to drive Gould to any club interested in buying him. So many people wanted to get up close and personal with him. Albion's John Kaye swung Gould by the neck in the dressing room, so did Coventry's John Sillett. Later, Frank Lampard Senior regularly put him in a headlock. Bristol City's manager Alan Dicks *"grappled with him"* in the bath, while Alan Ross of Carlisle was sent off for punching the striker.

The Albion Board interviewed him with a degree of desperation as their first, second and third choices were clear they wanted no part of the Hawthorns. Gould does have personal charisma, and this was key in persuading a majority of the six-man Board that he was the right person for the job. Being thick skinned, having a willingness to take flak or even a punch were considered valuable assets too. *"He was brilliant at interview"* one director confessed to me years later. His major talent was in spotting talent, previously overlooked players from lower Divisions or Non-League who could be sold on for a profit.

Gould could point to his success in keeping flat-broke and homeless Bristol Rovers in the Third Division. Interesting club, Rovers – among Gould's players were Gary Mabbutt, Tony Pulis, Keith Curle and Ian Holloway, which made for interesting tactical discussions. Their Chief Executive was Gordon Bennett, a genuine Rovers nut, who dealt stoically with problems like having one hour to fill a furniture van with club possessions before the gates of Eastville were locked. There was only so much lunacy Gordon could take and eventually moved to Albion as Club Secretary. He quickly learnt that unorthodox activities weren't confined to the West Country.

Another factor was Gould's willingness to work with all of Albion's rather large squad. John Silk again: *"Bobby Gould is a sensible chap. Many managers when they join a club take a dislike to certain players. Gould will give everyone an opportunity."*

Appointing Gould was a big gamble for the Board, and, perhaps, partial retaliation to being railroaded into appointing Brian Talbot. Supporter power and five straight wins got "Big Nose" the job despite misgivings at the top. Over a whisky (or several) in the oak-lined room, it's easy to imagine the gang of six persuading themselves that the opinion of the "great unwashed" wasn't worth considering. *"They wanted Talbot and look what happened..."*

At the press conference to announce his arrival, Silk naively admitted that Gould was not his first choice. Sometimes truth needs more economy. The Chairman was a first rate solicitor but the Court Room was a world away from professional football and its disparate, unchecked opinions. Silk cut an elderly, uninspiring and defensive figure and as he admitted to me much later: *"I'm a solicitor. I was bought up in an era where solicitors didn't sell themselves. They couldn't. They could be struck off if they touted for business. When I was standing for election to the Board, I found it difficult to sell myself. I found the idea rather uncouth."*

The Chairman's conference confession provided ammunition for the critics. The letter pages in the Argus were filled with protests around "lack of ambition" (*"are the Board deaf?"* asked Alan Clements, a well-known Baggies regular) and the new manager had lost his honeymoon period. In my own Argus column, I highlighted all the supporters' concerns and concluded *"And to the Board I say "on your heads be it. If this appointment doesn't succeed, there will be nobody to blame but yourselves."* During this period, the Argus was a major shaper of supporter opinions, selling 60,000 copies across the conurbation.

The Grorty Dick editorial that month was a plea from the heart. *"The more you care about this club, the greater the urge to retire to a quiet place and scream. We are asked, we are pleaded with, to support the club by people who clearly don't know best, but think they do. Our frustrations are made sandpaper raw by having no input into the club or having sensible suggestions ignored. They won't listen and they won't explain while the Hawthorns is metaphorically burning down."*

Public Relations – what public relations? Diplomacy, basic communications - call it what you will – the constant lack of these smoothing aids constantly ate away at the club in 1991, and those who supported it. Local media men Malcolm Boyden and Steve Tudgay had reputations to build and their sabre thrusts cruelly underlined Albion's collective and individual shortcomings. Albion were too impoverished, or didn't have the foresight, to employ anyone with PR or newspaper experience. It was folly. The manager quickly learnt that: *"if you say something off the record it can be abused by certain journalists..."*

Don Howe warned Gould not to take the job, presumably based on his experience a mere 16 years earlier. Gould had huge respect for Howe, although he was probably the only person with Albion connections who did. As Sutton Baggie Gary Elwell pointed out *"Don Howe says he is a good manager. That is no recommendation at all."*

In our collective angst, few pondered just how hard the Albion managers' job would be for anyone. Beyond the relegation concerns and lack of funds, there were many agendas behind-the-scenes. The Board was split, and thus any decision-making was long-winded and painful. Gould and Pearson didn't get on, though, in public at least, pretended otherwise. (This wasn't unusual, as by his own admission, Gould rarely saw eye-to-eye with any assistant at any club.) Club Captain Roberts was peeved he didn't get the job, and was already looking for his next move.

Albion was a highly disunited ship. The team as a whole were inconsistent, and were notorious for losing concentration at crucial moments. *"It seems that players at this club have a physiological barrier to get through"* the new Boss later mused. The aggressive local media were poised to dissect every action. Worse, there was little talent to draw upon from the routinely underfunded reserve and youth teams though to his credit, "the man from Coventry" genuinely gave hopefuls more opportunities than any other manager since. On top of that, the club's rich history is a burden for an incoming manager, not a blessing. Current players are invariably compared with their illustrious predecessors. Gould had no previous experience of running a "big" club.

There was an early indication the new manager was rather different. He confessed on his second day in charge, he'd gone in search of Dudley Town FC and ended up in Brierley Hill instead. His words were not picked up at the time yet they were a portent of his eccentric nature. On the other hand, his opening address to the local hacks betrayed a rare imagination. *"I'm not here to bore people. It's about building a club from within and giving people a belief and understanding and belonging to a football club."*

Albion's first match under the new Boss was at home against leaders West Ham. The match ended in a creditable 0-0 draw with everything possible done to avoid any mention of "hump-ball" such as all our large forwards being confined to the bench. After that, WBA suffered six straight defeats. They lost by a single goal at promotion chasing Sheffield Wednesday, then went down cruelly 2-1 on a plastic pitch in the 95th minute to another top side - Oldham.

But otherwise, there were no real excuses. Each defeat built more pressure. Even the die-hards were in despair following another setback at imitation Albion in late March. *"This night by Christ for a WBA fan was one of pain, wistfulness – and fear"* thundered author Richard Brentnall. *"The raindrops dripping off our nose on the open terrace could have been tears."* The gallant few who had travelled purely in hope, and had only wet clothes to take home, deserved better. A nine point safety margin over the bottom two (only two clubs would be relegated that season) the club enjoyed upon Gould's appointment was whittled down to zero.

Without the injured Goodman, WBA could not score. Bannister and West had reasonable scoring record under Talbot but playing the Gould way were completely unable to find the net. Throwing in young Les Palmer from the reserves wasn't the answer either.

Gould gambled on three new players, namely striker Paul Williams from Stockport, plus midfielders Winston White and Kwame Ampadu on deadline day, just before a visit to Charlton. At the time, the Londoners were reluctant tenants at Selhurst Park. The "squatters" (as they were known by Palace fans) were a mid-table side yet easily outplayed the new-look Albion side, winning 2-0. The visiting support, already obliged to sit down at an expensive £8 per head as the terraces were closed, were unimpressed. Some made V-signs at the Albion players, and booed when the team applauded them at the end. The majority of the away support chose not to respond at all. Albion had scored only twice in Gould's first seven games.

At a pre-arranged gathering of London and West Midlands based Baggies at a nearby pub, there was a collective determination to get gloriously drunk to ease the hurt. Most succeeded, famously including Richard Brentnall, who headed for the toilet and fell off a first floor balcony instead. Everyone rushed to his assistance, but Ritchie got up immediately and dusted himself down, completely unhurt. Overall, the vast alcohol consumption added some much-needed perspective, but only until the next match. No-one knew at the time, but the noisy, depressed group of supporters had just witnessed Albion's last defeat of the season. One of the talking points was the solo performance by one supporter in Selhurst Park. Singing unaccompanied and loudly, he launched into a Baggies version of *"I Believe."* It was completely original, spontaneous and rather fanciful, but such efforts deserved applause and that's exactly what he got plus *"I'll have what he's having…"*

The football club had to extend their overdraft to cover their "new talent." Ampadu was a loanee, but Winston White at £25,000 cost the equivalent of half a home gate, and Paul Williams at £250,000 equalled roughly 25% of all gate takings for a season. It was another gamble (or back-covering) by the Board. The new blood could have made the difference. But they didn't. To this day, the story that Gould bought the wrong Paul Williams. Stockport had two, the other being a decent full back. There is a convincing school of thought this was the worst ever transfer business in recent memory, although the fees were tiny compared to two decades later.

None of the bedraggled supporters heading unsteadily towards the train station at Selhurst would have believed they'd endured their final defeat of the season. Albion finally turned their fortunes around three days later by beating Swindon 2-1, ironically on April Fools' Day. With nothing happening up front, despite a bold looking 3-4-3 formation, defenders Roberts (with a late-ish penalty) and Steve Parkin won the game. It was a timely boost, not least because the return fixture against the Tatters was next. Among the sparse Swindon attendance was Dave Watkin, an IT project manager from Kingswinford. He hasn't missed an Albion game since, home or away.

Molineux looked sad. Yes, nothing changes there, but on this occasion, the place was particularly sad because it was an unlikely two-sided ground. Apart from the new double-decker John Ireland stand (later to find fame as the 'gobbing gallery') the only other area deemed "safe" was the huge South Bank terrace. At half-time, the 4,000 away supporters were pelted with lumps of concrete from those lovable Tatters. In what became a classic Argus misprint, the reporter noted: *"thankfully no-one was insured."* It wasn't even factually correct, as bleeding Albion supporters sought medical assistance. Our players were racially abused, including Goodman who had the satisfaction of scoring in a 2-2 draw. The Tatters had a defender in goal for much of the game after Stowell had been carried off. Not for the first time this season, it felt like an opportunity missed.

A knackered-looking Steve Bull again got little change out of the old warrior Graham Roberts. Albion's skipper had been tipped off in advance, so was unsurprised when a supporter ran on the pitch to present him with a carrot. Roberts joked later about saving money on feed for his horses. He was probably rather more surprised when Bobby Gould ran on and manhandled the supporter off the pitch. *"I made a citizen's arrest"* explained the manager later. His intervention was aiming at removing a distraction and focussing attention on beating the Tatters. In vain. Just to give our discomfort a final twist, there was no segregation outside the ground. The consequences were predictable.

Two home matches followed against fellow strugglers. Despite battering rock-bottom Hull, the visitors escaped with a draw. Albion, playing a bold 3-4-3 formation, did everything bar score. Some supporters wanted a target for their frustrations and goalkeeper Mel Rees was the new scapegoat. Rather like the infamous Paul Crichton years later, the more Rees was criticised, the more ineffectual became his contribution. No-one knew that two years later Rees would be dead, taken by bowel cancer at the early age of 26.

In the "must win" game against Leicester, Albion did just that, though left it very late. Goodman's 93rd minute winner was virtually sucked into the net by a thoroughly stirred-up Brummie Road. In the first half, there was a Brummie Road cry of *"Bobby, Bobby, give us a wave..."* The manager duly obliged. That same weekend, an Argus letter writer argued that *"Gould was the best appointment since Ron Atkinson in*

1977." It's possible the letter was a spoof. It takes one to know one – I'd written many spoofs to the Argus over the years myself.

However, the result was everything and the Baggies manager was genuinely winning some people over. It's easy to mock as part of a mob, but less difficult on a one to one basis. Gould was a guest at the then-thriving Gloucestershire Branch, run by the Bishop of Gloucester (that's John Bishop of Fourbuoys newsagents), an easy trip from his rented Worcestershire cottage. Gould proved to be a popular guest, taking all critical comments on the chin, while managing to sound articulate, passionate and honest. Gould's eloquence impressed all the self-styled "farmers".

Further exploiting the Supporters Club network would have boosted his credibility (Denis Smith, for example, visited 7 branches in just a few months), but WBASC London Branch, for one, were vexed by his unwillingness to visit them.

A new enthusiasm was building that we would survive (the *"I Believe"* chant was heard at every game) using the flexible 3-4-3 line-up. Gould stuck with it at Oakwell against a decent-looking Barnsley. The away following numbered an impressive 3,000, and other than a collective dig at Mel Rees (again), there was much positive noise from an open terrace. The manager worked the empathy card by highlighting: *"that the supporters had sucked Strodder's equaliser over the line. "*

There was one sour note. According to the Barnsley tannoy (who were tipped off by the Albion), Bristol Rovers would sell tickets direct to WBA supporters for the last match of the season. It was simply bizarre, and dangerously wrong.

Days later, WBA were on the road again – this time to Watford for an ugly scrap between two of the bottom three. Travelling the same road were an extraordinary 5,000 Albion supporters. Their collective Baggie-backing determination led to almighty traffic jams with the usual last resort of abandoning cars anywhere. Fortunately, the local law enforcement officers had the night off (unlike later visits). Hundreds of away supporters jogged uphill at various speeds between the allotments to get inside before kick-off.

The match was frantic. "Bruiser" Naylor was back between the sticks, and was warmly received, partly because he wasn't Rees. Goodman gave us the lead when he beat David James (yes, that one). Although Roeder quickly levelled, Albion tried to keep the ball in the face of near-naked intimidation and came close to winning. But the priority was not to lose. In the last minute, Albion won a corner but Gould kept his big defenders back in their own half. His caution was not well received in the away end. Just one more goal and history could have been so different...

The run of saggy draws weren't enough to move the Baggies out of the danger zone and now only three very tense games remained – two of them at home. The first of these against Port Vale was to become infamous.

Albion won a joke penalty. First choice taker Graham Roberts was unfit, so new boy Paul Williams, desperate to score his first goal, volunteered to take the spot kick. He wildly banged the ball high over the crossbar. Afterwards, he confessed; *"my whole game fell apart."* Less generous supporters didn't notice the difference and hurled abuse at the Irishman.

Famously, the Baggies secured another generous penalty. Fans favourite Goodman strode forward to take it. Donno was the 'man'. We'd be OK now ... but Goodman could only hit a fan rather than the net. It's quite impossible to describe the screaming frustration of the Hawthorns faithful. Didn't they want to stay up?

Albion did try to make amends and to immense relief, Goodman equalised and then scored the winner. Or everyone thought he did. The referee, deciding he'd been far too generous, disallowed the second goal. To this day and, after endless replays, it's still impossible to understand why.

Albion had just one meagre point to show for their efforts amid wails, curses and gnashed teeth.

When cornered by the media, Chairman John Silk sought to distance the Board from blame by pointing out that *"he didn't miss the penalties against Port Vale".* The hasty words became infamous, sounding both negative and far from the spirit of "we're in this together."

Silk was such an easy target. He was also asked to comment on Gould signing a two-year contract to which he responded: *"I am delighted with his management of the club since he arrived."* Mischievously, the local press implied that Gould's indifferent results had been rewarded with a better deal .In reality, Gould had only agreed a contract in principle upon joining and this was the final deal.

The Baggies were horribly nervous in their final home League match against Newcastle United. In theory, the mid-table Geordies had nothing to play for but this wasn't quite true. The United players had a new manager to impress – one Ossie Ardiles. Don Goodman gave the home side the lead with a spectacular free kick but then hobbled off with a re-occurrence of his hamstring injury. *Did our season die with that 'hammy'?* Gould opted to put another midfielder on the pitch and revert to 4-5-1 with Paul Williams the hapless lone front runner. Although WBA dominated, they rarely looked like scoring again and predictably conceded an equaliser. The remaining time was played out in an agonising stalemate, the pressure evident with every pass.

It's curious how Ardiles' contribution to our demise is always overlooked. Had his youthful team (including one Andrew Hunt) strolled half-heartedly through proceedings, Albion's short-term destiny would have been very different. However "If only" was a re-occurring theme throughout the season, such as the missed penalties against Port Vale.

Still, hope remained for our rattled ranks. Relegation rivals Leicester City lost, so Albion had their fate within their own hands. If they beat Bristol Rovers in the last game, they would stay up. Any other outcome and they needed a favour from Leicester's opponents, Oxford United.

The natives were very restless. With 28 years of active support behind her, Glynis Harrison was distraught: "*I had previously believed that Third Division football at the Hawthorns was about as likely as the Reverend Ian Paisley attending Mass. Well in recent times, I have had to revise my opinions somewhat. I want to howl in frustrated rage, a howl the reverberations of which will be felt in the Board Room, dressing room and manager's office for with each succeeding match the bone-chilling thought gets stronger; it will be a long time, if ever, before I see top flight football at the Hawthorns again.*" Glynis was clear on one point: "*I sincerely believe Gould will be the salvation of the Baggies.*" Cynical reader, I still married her although admittedly I did invite Bobby Gould to the ceremony.

Bath. Twerton Park. Bristol Rovers. Even now, a whole generation of fans find those words and phrases hurtful and gut-twisting. Only the passage of 25 years permits some analysis of that eventful day without raw emotion taking over. Bath being a Roman town, the theme of "Togas at Rovers" was one of Dean Walton's more imaginative ideas, apparently stemming from supping Guinness on the pre-season Irish tour. The idea was well received, and it was said there wasn't a Roman Legionnaire's costume to be had in any Black Country costume hire shop.

The first cohort of Black Country Legionnaires hit Bath at
opening time (then 11 o'clock). Locals and visitors alike
gaped at the spectacle. A party of Dutch tourists were first to
reach for their cameras. The show was up and running.
Allocating only 1,200 tickets for the visitors was simply
pathetic, given the importance of the game and this
contributed to our ultimate downfall. Had capacity not been an
issue, we'd have outnumbered the Rovers mob two or more to
one and marginalised their influence. But in a tiny 7,500
capacity non-League venue, this advantage was negated.
Albion supporters can be very resourceful. Some found legal
(or not so legal) ways onto the home terraces. To do so was
particularly challenging, given the Police road blocks on all the
surrounding streets. People with Black Country accents
waved money at the startled owners of neighbouring houses
to stand in their back garden, or even at their bedroom
windows. Turnstile operators were offered increasingly large
sums of money without success. And all the time, there was
the risk of being attacked by Rovers supporters. Albion
people in fancy dress were assaulted at the station, in the
town and near the ground. The atmosphere was quite hateful.
Around 200 Albion supporters managed to get into the home
end. Sutton Branch stalwart Amanda Hume (then Miles) was
one of them, with her then boyfriend Neville: *"We got to the
ground extremely early and took up an excellent vantage point
on the home terraces, immediately above the halfway line. As*

kick-off approached, we could hear some Albion fans had got into our stand and were noisily making their way towards where we were standing. As luck would have it, they met the equally voluble Rovers' fans within a few yards of us and then it all started. Punches were flying, fans were rolling around, kicking and fighting one another and the Police stood passively on the pitch, observing without moving. I was all for sticking it out as I didn't want to lose my great view when the match started but Neville kept telling me that we had to move. I resisted until a punch swished past his ear and, at that point, he offered me no choice and shoved me under the crash barrier and onto the pitch to escape the melee. We retreated to a safer distance where we were "entertained" by a local who kept referring to 'Bobby Gould's bum-boys' for some strange reason."

Amanda had an additional anxiety *"Footage of those crowd scenes was shown on News at Ten later that week to illustrate that hooliganism was still alive and there I was as plain as the nose on the end of your face. I hadn't dared tell my mother about what had happened but amazingly she never spotted me. Yet a friend who was also watching that night saw me, and ribbed me next day for my part in this national disgrace."*

As a concession, Bath Police encouraged hundreds of ticketless supporters to stand on a grass bank, partially overlooking the ground. Ground? "Trumpton" didn't even compare well with many Non-League stadia. *"The sort of place that evoked visions of guards taking prisoners for their daily exercise"* suggested rookie Albion follower Ian Hall. The away terrace felt distinctly cage-like - narrow, ugly and with a big fence separating supporters from pitch. As if to maximise the inconvenience, a line of Police and stewards stood in front, with mounted Police nearby. Not only supporters were struggling to see much. So many hacks needed entry that several ended up on the terrace, with a crush barrier to support their note-taking.

The manager's' team selection defied football common sense. It's unforgiveable that in such a vital match, the Albion team selection was so wrong. Paul Williams still hadn't scored, but Gould considered that his pairing with another target man in

Colin West would comprise the Albion forward line. They'd never played together competitively before. The club's top goal scorer, Gary Bannister, was on the bench. 19 year old striker Adrian Foster, with one game to his name, would also start – in midfield. At the back, young Darren Rogers made only his third appearance. Of course, the manager knew his senior professionals were not performing well. So he gambled with kids and players out of position... and failed.

Yet it all started so well. Rovers' biggest signing Carl Saunders was sent off in the 3rd minute for elbowing Raven. In theory, that dismissal should have turned the game. But Rovers' pumped-up ten men and their supporters were on a mission to bring down Gould. Their cheaply assembled side (costing £90,000) was mid-table and had only that focus in mind.

Few Albionites at the time could appreciate the depths of hatred aimed at Gould from Rovers though in the subsequent year, many more would come to think the same way. Gould had managed Rovers three times, and chosen to leave each time. He'd subsequently been banned from their training ground for a remark he made as a TV reporter. The players he left behind remembered some of his bizarre motivation techniques, and not necessarily in a fond manner.

The lopsided Albion team couldn't settle, and the first half was largely a stalemate. But we had to score. Leicester were beating Oxford 1-0, and relegation was beckoning. Adrian Foster had a shot kicked off the line just before half-time. With barely 20 minutes left, it was Foster again, clear with the ball at his feet just six yards from goal ... and keeper Parkin knocked his shot around the post. Two minutes later, Rovers scored and our world fell in.

 Now the Baggies needed two goals. They struggled to manage one despite a belated appearance from Gary Bannister. Rovers put everybody behind the ball. In injury time, Ampadu's low cross eluded everyone and sneaked into the net through a crowd of legs. A group of Albion supporters celebrated from their vantage point on top of an advertising hoarding in the home end. There was brief elation with the news that Oxford had equalised at Filbert Street, a goal which would have saved the Baggies but it was disallowed. There was no time to score again. Albion were relegated to the third tier for the first time ever.

"What a way to treat your fans" was a heartfelt bitter cry from the away terraces after the whistle.   The pitch was full of rampaging Rovers supporters in goading mood. Only the fence and the Police prevented a mass brawl. It was wrong to respond, but rationality had long been torn away - together with many "togas." Photographers were hovering like vultures, exploiting our misery. One homed in on a tearful young Teresa Hill from Tipton and her image quickly became iconic.

The path to the toilets was within shouting distance of the so-called executive areas where the Albion directors lurked. There were a lot of shouts and much anger. Trying to go one better, veteran supporters' Paul Dubberley and Kevin Secker headed for the dressing room to vent their anger. Others had already tried and failed, but much to their own surprise, the door was open so they went in. Their astonishment was so acute that they forgot all their prepared choice words. Bobby Gould quickly showed them the door he said: *"Get out lads, you know how the team must feel."* In rational times, there were numerous retorts available but words failed the pair and they left. Had they lingered, they may have heard the former Rovers man tell his players that some of them didn't have enough 'investment' in the club. In his 16 games, Gould had just two victories to his name.

Gould's brave or foolish reliance on youth was only a boost for Leicester City. Neither Darren Rogers (who was honest enough to admit *"the situation got to me"*) nor Adrian Foster were to have much of a professional career. Six years later, a now-experienced Foster was involved in another "shit or bust" match, when either Hereford United or Brighton would drop out of the Football League. Foster, wearing the black and white of the Bulls, missed a glorious chance five minutes from time. As a result, United were relegated, not to return for nine years. Some players just can't handle the big occasion. Maybe he'd never fully recovered from following Wolves as a kid.

Meanwhile, John Silk was digging another hole for himself.

"At the end of the game, microphones were thrust at me. One chap was saying that it would be tough going in the Third Division and I replied that if we did well, we would get better gates and we could buy more players. Then when another microphone was immediately thrust in my face, I said the same thing about getting better gates in the Third Division, not realising that the same question had not been asked of me again. And so "we'll get better gates in the Third Division" came out by itself. My faux pas."

Author Richard Brentnall: "As far as football grounds go, Twerton Park to be sure, is the Dump to end all Dumps. But the real dump of that day wasn't a noun, a farmyard posing as a stadium; it was a verb, the dumping of the Albion and its truly fine supporters into a nightmare scenario by the gormless people who have overseen the seven-year strangulation of the Throstle with an incompetence such that might well have purposely wrung it's neck themselves. "

Glynis Harrison: "My head was a shed, an empty one. Like a radio station that had closed down for the night, the carrier wave was there, but of the programme, nothing. I looked around, all I saw was a toga-clad sea of broken, beaten faces. It's not pleasant either seeing good Black Country blokes weeping tears of bitter despair. Seeing Baggie people I know well reduced to that. Richard Brentnall in particular, resting against a crash barrier looking like he'd been simultaneously hit by a half-end brick, and Hamlet's ghost. Images. The scene struck a chord in my memory – where had I seen the same thing before? Then I remembered the old newsreels. All our Yesterdays, an ITV programme broadcast a long time ago. I was a child, they were featuring 1940 – Dunkirk, and General Gort's battle weary troops looking much the same as they disembarked from the little boats. I was witnessing it again, Albion's Dunkirk. "

Richard Brentnall again: "So there I stood, five o'clock, forlorn buses for company. Somehow numb at that moment as stark reality of it wrestled together on the battleground of my mind. A gaze up to the heavens for clarity. Then the images. My boyhood, and a steward named Fred Ashley from Smethwick who'd smuggle me in to watch Kevan and the rest. Chippy

Clark, Astle, May '68. Willie Johnston scorching a trail with his fists clenched. Big Wiley giving blood. Cunningham using Old Trafford as a dance-floor and Regis bursting nets. A standing salute in Valencia, muting 95,000 in Belgrade. Unfulfilled hopes. The nearly men.   And now – the nowhere men, How the f++++ could it be allowed to sink to this? Then I stood and suddenly I could feel my chin quivering and that my cheeks were wet. "

Glynis again: *"Much to my surprise, I didn't shed tears. I simply entered into a state of shock, exacerbated by a considerable intake of alcohol that night. On the way back, we paused at the Greyhound pub near Gloucester, where we bumped into a posse of Potters en-route post-match from Stoke." Welcome to the Third Division," they said. It wasn't a hostile gesture; they genuinely felt for our plight, as we quaffed ale and commiserated well into the night. We did discover a mutual enmity of Wolves which felt like consolation to while away the hours we were in our cups."*

Then Mail journalist and Baggie follower Jeff Prestridge summed up the view of many. *"Relegation hurts like hell. I thought Albion had a divine right to remain in the top echelons of the Football League."*

"Relegation hurt" agreed former keeper John Osborne. *"I suppose it's a matter of pride. It doesn't mean so much telling my grandson that I played for WBA. I used to think it was one of a half a dozen clubs it couldn't happen to."* Famously, the King himself, Jeff Astle, was in the away end, and his views simply weren't repeatable.

There was yet more injury on top of insult. That night, 200 so-called Albion supporters gave us all a bad name by taking out their frustrations on property and people in Weston Super Mare.

1991-92 Coffin for Gould?

So much hurt and rage to get out and only friends to dump on in those pre-internet, pre-mobile phone days. Thus the first friendly match in July was cathartic. Albion folk needed to be with their own, the only other people who understood and talk through the issues over a pint or six. The officials of Dudley Town, in their temporary ramshackle Round Oak premises, were overwhelmed, but rather grateful for a new ground attendance record. Apart from putting the world to rights, there was the need for reassurance that the team and management wanted out of this Division as much as we did.

It was clear at Dudley that most supporters saw the Third Division only as a constant source of shame, a devil despoiler of club history which needed exorcising. Supporters' legend Dean Walton was a rare exception: *"Personally, I am eagerly looking forward to the new season, especially the away trips, lots of new grounds to see Albion play on, numerous new pubs to visit, and new acquaintances to be made – because to me, this is what football is all about, not just the 90 minutes (which is usually crap!) but the whole occasion. Our away match crowd consists of a great bunch of mates who only get*

together on a Saturday, and we have certainly had some good times, win, lose or draw.

Home matches could be the worst part – a cold January night match against the likes of Hartlepool etc doesn't present much of an attraction, but even then there are the couple of pints in the Woodman to look forward to, and the next away trip to plan." There was admirable maturity in Deano's thoughts (how often over the years have we said "great day, shame about the football in the middle?") but few wanted to consider such thoughts at the time.

Days later nearly 3,000 Baggies descended on the Grove, home of Halesowen Town FC and locust –like, drank the place dry. It was a low-key friendly on a soporific warm day. Having been taken by surprise at Dudley, the Police turned up en masse in four transit vans, and on horseback, like unwanted wedding guests. They soon found useful work to do, insisting that Albion fans all had to queue at the same turnstiles, while others remained unused. Inside, there was no segregation.

Due to lack of interest from other clubs, on display was essentially the same squad that finished the previous season. Understandably, Gould needed fresh talent, and transfer-listed most of the squad, including Strodder, Robson and Raven, but few clubs were willing to match their existing salaries. Gould's job was already horribly difficult.

Let's spell it out: West Bromwich Albion owed almost £2 million of which over half was owed to Barclays Bank. Total club income for the previous season was £2.2 million. Common perception had a divided Board, led by an elderly, far-from-dynamic Chairman. In addition, there was a hostile press, expectant supporters and a large squad of players, with no security of employment and little knowledge of the Third Division. All of these factors didn't help promotion potential. The stubborn counter-argument from the terraces was simply that our well-paid, experienced second tier men ought to thrive in the Third Division. We had continuity with five of the squad having over 100 Albion games to their names. After all, the bookies had WBA at 6/1 favourites to win the title and we did have Don Goodman, surely the best striker in the Division.

The main man was indeed fit again but elsewhere there was only a short-term loanee goalkeeper – Alan Miller from Arsenal, to add any freshness to the starting X1. Gould did secure cheap youngsters Hanson and Heggs for the future. Somehow it was appropriate that Gould should sign the rather eccentric Heggs.

There was one painful summer exit. Following a petty dispute over wages, young Ugo Ehiogu accepted an approach from Aston Villa. The spat, over a £10 increase, illustrated to the manager just what he was up against. Villa admitted an illegal approach at a tribunal, were duly fined and a massive sell-on clause imposed but at the end of the day, the Seals had helped themselves to a major Albion asset. Much later, this sell-on was hugely helpful to Gary Megson but for Gould, this was just another pain in his posterior to endure.

Meanwhile, newspaper headlines featured plans for top-flight clubs to break away to form a "Super League." There were suggestions that the new League would remain exclusive meaning no promotion or relegation. London Baggie Duncan Jones summed up our concerns *"at a time when football is changing hopefully for the better, we are in danger of being left behind permanently."*

Elsewhere, there were more official restrictions on what we could or couldn't do as supporters. The Football (Offences) Act 1991 made invading the pitch, throwing missiles towards the pitch, and racist chanting all criminal offences.

In an attempt to (literally) build bridges; Albion's pre-season get-away consisted of a week at an army training camp. It was certainly cheap, an important consideration for a club where every penny counted, but it was hard to find many other positives.

The surprising wave of enthusiasm or, more likely, the instinctive need for Throstles to flock together, resulted in an unlikely increase in season ticket sales. Over 4,000 supporters paid up front for another season of fun and frolics. Better still, almost 13,000 turned up for the opening-day battle with newly-promoted Exeter. Less welcome were 52 Police officers, whose presence cost Albion six grand.

"Always look on the bright side of life" had its first Brummie

Road airing. Most of the attendance 'got it'. Whatever the result, Albion would finish the day in their lowest ever League position. The cry was much mocked by the cider-slurping visitors, both during the game and later in their excellent fanzine, the Exe-Directory.

The City fanzine dedicated much copy to their thoughts on WBA, underpinned by their OTT argument that City were the new kids on the block, and us the tired old lags. The thoughts of one correspondent were typical: *"I wondered about "this lost in the past" mentality that Birmingham, West Brom and Stoke seem to exhibit. They really do seem to believe they're better than the rest of us and we should all be grateful for the chance to play them. Well I bloody well hope we're still playing them next season. Let's hear it lads ... "You're not famous, you're not famous, you're not famous any more."* The accusation of arrogance from fans of other clubs was to become a familiar one over the season.

Much to everyone's surprise, Albion's 2-1 half-time lead stretched to an impressive-sounding 6-3 final score. Exeter players were hyped-up (had they read the fanzine?) and lunged recklessly at their opponents and it cost them two first half penalties – both coolly despatched by Craig Shakespeare. Even though Goodman was substituted to preserve his limbs, the goalfest continued and even Paul Williams found the net in his 11th game. His header found the bottom corner, and he looked very pleased indeed. Briefly, he could laugh off the jibes that his (Noble Peace prize-winning) mother was more famous than he was. The season had started on a high, and the noisy insults from the Devonians in the Rainbow Stand were laughed off.

Albion's first away League game was a classic "welcome to the Third Division" at Darlington. Ancient Feethams was owned by neighbours Darlington Cricket Club and to access the tiny ground meant a walk around the boundary of the cricket pitch. One set of turnstiles served both clubs.

Barely a year earlier, 'Darlo' were in the Conference. Managed by Brian Little, they'd gone up as Champions and followed that by winning the Fourth Division Play-Offs with a notoriously negative style of football. And now they were playing WBA in a League match.

The only part of the ground with a fence was, inevitably the away terrace, with an eight foot high monstrosity. The wretched grill was installed for a one-off visit from Middlesbrough a few years earlier but was retained, even in the Conference.

The match was all ticket for visitors (limited to 1,200) but not for home supporters. I stood on a home terrace with the Darlington fanzine editor, and a mutual friend who supported Middlesbrough, but few other Albion people followed my low-key example. More happily, Albion fans rated the catering as excellent, even if it was comically served from a Mister Whippy ice cream van clone.

With intelligence from their Bath and Weston-Super-Mare colleagues, the local plods were highly visible. The invasive activities of one Police video team created resentment among the innocent drinking groups in Darlo town centre. It was unfortunate the eager film crew were nowhere to be seen after the match, when several Albion supporters were hit with fists or stones.

Albion wore their new and very bright red and yellow striped outfit. Opinions were mixed. For some, anything associated with Gould, however obliquely, could never be positive, whereas others such as Richard Brentnall were more positive. *"I like them, yellow and green always conjured up anachronistic images of Giles and Wile, Cunningham and Statham, glory days that are long gone. Let's look the future in the eye."* Bobby Gould claimed credit for the Melchester Rovers lookalike. The choice was deliberate as *"red is a dominant and intimidatory colour."* Perhaps he'd just spent too long at Bristol Rovers.

Albion, with striker Gary Piggott making his League debut at 22, were definitely the stronger side but the twin pressures of dealing with Darlington's formidable defence, and supporter's expectations, saw many chances come and go. The solitary goal came very late from Don Goodman, neatly set up by Paul Williams. The celebrations were more about relief than joy. All decent so far, but Goodman was injured again and we know what happens in his absence, don't we children? The next match was drawn, and the barracking began. What Albion managers want and what supporters want are not always the same. The paying public wanted out of the Third Division quickly, and they expected their team to win by playing football on the grass. The team soon appreciated the gap between these expectations and their own abilities. Patience, in short supply since May, ran out at Fulham, a side who'd just avoided the Fourth Division the previous term. The Londoners looked like a relegation-threatened side. So too did Albion, who seemed quite unable to impose themselves. An away following of 1,200, despite being a midweek fixture, were narked by a goalless draw, bellowing repeatedly: *"We Want Football"*. The fanzine match reporter noted: *"the only way in which anyone could have been at all spellbound by this match was through the degree of its constant appallingness."* The infamous long ball was much in evidence.

"*It was an amazing experience, and we were all staggered by the reaction of supporters to a 0-0 draw away from home"* explained the manager. That night, we saw another side of Gould and his first "motivational" tactic. Re-using an idea he'd previously inflicted on his Rovers team, he ordered the entire squad to the large away terrace to applaud those who were jeering them. The tactic backfired. We continued to collectively hurl abuse at the players, who tried gamely to muster a modicum of interest. Understandably, the players felt let down by the manager for not backing them. From their point of view, the club were unbeaten in 13 League matches and they considered they were doing a decent professional job. As Ampadu explained: *"it's not a nice feeling to have your own supporters screaming and shouting at you throughout the second half and at the final whistle. I've never known anything like it before."*

Neither Ampadu nor any of his team mates touched on how ill-prepared they were for the match. Gould had again inflicted Jallalabad Barracks on his reluctant squad. They'd travelled to the barracks on Monday, and stayed overnight before travelling to Fulham on Tuesday. As Captain Shakespeare pointed out; *"it was crazy preparation. I had one of the worst night's sleep of my life in that army cot."*

The result was disappointing, but it wasn't awful. With the cooling impact of hindsight, the vitriol was a hangover from the desperate pain of last season, a lingering bitterness that the club's cherished history was being rubbed in the dirt. The few supporters allowed into Twerton had had little opportunity to vent their spleen. The manager tried to justify his actions later: *"I made the players stand on the pitch. It was important we listened to the angry message from the fans. It amounted to a demonstration and I wanted my players to listen and understand the passion that led to it."*

Rather than inspiring the Stars in Stripes, their next performance was even worse. For the 2,000+ who travelled to Bolton, this fixture stood out for its sheer awfulness. Burnden Park was never a welcoming venue, a big old-fashioned ground with a spectacular drop between pitch and the surrounding stands. The front of the terracing was level with the players' feet. The stadium was simply too big for the Wanderers so, to ease their money worries, they sold part of one end to a supermarket. The remaining open corner section was ample for most away support, although the building obscured the view of one corner flag.

Gould's line-up was "bold", pairing the youthful Adrian Foster with Gary Piggott as our strike force, leaving old lags Williams and Bannister on the bench. A supporter survey several years later rated them as the worst forward line that Albion had *ever* fielded. Cynics suggested the pairing was deliberate so that we could better appreciate the merits of Paul Williams. Certainly, probably for the only time, there were urgent appeals to get Williams onto the pitch. WBA mustered only 3 shots in 90 minutes, at the time considered a very meagre return.

Bolton were only average themselves, but in central midfield they had Tony "the Belly" Kelly, a Ron Saunders folly who, could barely get into an Albion shirt. Kelly played when he felt like it, and made his point by setting up the third in a one-sided 3-0 defeat. It was a metaphorical two-fingered gesture to both WBA and their supporters. A couple of years earlier, having written a factual statement that the midfielder was overweight, I was taken aback to be confronted by the man himself in Halfords Lane. Kelly let rip, swearing and threatening. Fortunately Andy Gray pulled him away before the scene turned really nasty.

That vitriol did accurately underscore the intolerant mood that afternoon. For outsiders, a first defeat in 14 League matches didn't seem grounds for protest but outsiders didn't endure Twerton.

As we shuffled out, one Bolton steward could be heard saying to his colleague *"Was that really West Brom?"* Just to give us all time for reflection, no-one was allowed to leave the car park for half an hour, in a 1990's version of kettling. It's only much later that I learnt that the Police were aware of an Albion "firm" in the away end and wanted to deter them seeking out Bolton supporters. But the delay made no difference, with 20 of the firm later arrested after an evening of fighting.

Meanwhile, the manager had another cunning plan, generally considered to be another player punishment. He invited startled journalists into the dressing room to directly question the players. Cue embarrassment all round as half-hearted queries were posed by red-faced hacks, and responses made in a similar desultory manner by irritated players. *"I can still remember what every player was wearing on his feet"* confessed the Mail journo Steve Tudgay later.

Gould explained in his biography: *"I thought it was progressive – a way of breaking down barriers and having more openness like they do in American sports."* More realistically, it was an attempt to get his own back on local football writers, particularly Tudgay, who Gould considered had been antagonistic in his reporting. If so, the move was ill-conceived as it only increased antipathy. Either way, the players felt they weren't getting the manager's backing or protection. Gary Strodder: *"Our fans had barracked us for the second game running. The atmosphere in the dressing room after was icy. The gaffer was bristling with fury for 20 minutes and then he bought the local press in. None of the players wanted to talk."*

Debate continues to this day on what was the lowest-ever point in the club history. This comprehensive defeat by Bolton, who were an ordinary Third Division club down on their luck, felt like the bottom of the barrel. But there were to be several more contenders.

Gallows humour was much to the fore that afternoon. *"We're so shit, it's unbelievable"* had regular airings, together with the rather cruel *"Foster for England"* a bit harsh to ridicule a local-born striker trying to make good. Young Adrian had Twerton associations, which didn't help. He may have only have half-realised it at the time, but his Albion career virtually ended that day. Perhaps it was in everyone's interest.

Foster was once a guest at an Albion supporters' match. During play, a stray pass headed towards him at a rate of knots. All heads turned to see how the professional would respond. Chest it down, or would he lift his foot to control the ball? He did neither, and the ball hit him between the legs. *"He's a professional?"* was the kindest remark from the opposition.

Slightly wiser counsel prevailed once everyone calmed down. As Walsall-based veteran supporter Cyril Randle pointed out *"Bobby Gould inherited these players in the main, and nobody else bit his hand off to buy any of them."* Writing in the Argus, a Mr Westwood of West Bromwich was also sagacious. *"I feel Albion supporters expect too much. Be patient."*

Defeat in Lancashire was followed by two much needed

decent home wins to raise everyone's spirits. The first saw League leaders Stockport County beaten, with Williams scoring the winner against his old club. The Cheshire side deserved to lose because of their kit, which resembled the after-effects of someone vomiting blackberries and custard. There was some doubt whether the match could go ahead after an arson attack on the Brummie Road the previous evening. Only frantic early morning repair work literally saved the day.

Little Chester City put our travails into perspective. Already badly supported and hard up, they were reluctantly playing at a temporary base at Macclesfield until their new stadium was ready. As a result, their average attendances were just above 1,000, and were very grateful that West Bromwich Albion were in town.

Excited by a new ground only 70 miles away, the Baggies were backed by 3,000 supporters. There were rumours that 'mine host' from the local pub, The Brambles, funded a fortnight's holiday on the strength of bar takings that day. Non-League "Macc" was swamped. Their toilets and catering provisions were geared up for a dozen visitors, not thousands and huge queues built up.

Alarm mounted as the two sides of the ground allocated to visitors became uncomfortably crowded, with more struggling to get in. The larger of the two terraces had a ten foot high grill with exits only at either end. Hillsborough was on our minds... But Chester had a plan. Their own supporters were brigaded together to free up more room. Most hospitable! By kick-off time, the so-called home supporters, all 800 of 'em, barely occupied one quarter of Moss Rose, with lusty Black Country accents everywhere else. Never had "*you're supposed to be at home*" had so much resonance. The experience was unique, and gave us a renewed perspective that with such extraordinary backing, WBA could not possibly remain at this level much longer. Behind one goal was a huge banner *"We are West Brom – who the hell are you?"* We perceived this as a defiant message in troubled times, though Chester's supporters probably muttered "*arrogant wot-its.*" The match was a high workrate, long ball, big throw-in battle, far from ideal for shortarses Gary Robson and Stewart Bowen in the Albion midfield whose opponents looked twice their size. After being mainly on the defensive, Daryl Burgess's late strike handed Gould's men an unexpected three points. A good-natured pitch invasion was inspired by Burge's glory run to the halfway line.

Winning against the odds always feels highly satisfying, which served as handy balm as the narrow roads out of Macc quickly ground to a frustrating halt. The West Bromwich Albion mobile refugee column became stationary other than the shuffling pedestrians either side of the road. Dozens of radios bought welcome news of defeats for our rivals and car springs rocked, horns sounded and Baggies on foot leapt skyward. *"We are top of the League, I said we are top of the League..."* could heard in ragged chorus all along the street. One supporter clambered through his sunroof and perched himself precariously on the car roof to join in. When times are perceived as hard, any positive is seized upon. One fanzine contributor summed up Macc *"Wonderful day out, great beer, last minute win, on the pitch, friendly locals, great novelty value."*

Meanwhile, Chester remained in the bottom four, and their 800 die-hards were held inside the ground. *That's hard.* City never truly recovered and only a supporter takeover two decades later maintained football in the ancient city. And we were complaining?

Albion maintained their top spot by defeating Hull at home and Bobby Gould was named as Manager of the Month. His team had only lost once in 18 League matches, normally cause for rampant mutual back-slapping. Not at The Hawthorns, where raw fury was only a defeat away - or maybe not even that. One regular lament, with Twerton still raw, was the baffling team selections. Forwards were often played in wide midfield, and vice versa. Another sore was the ongoing disagreement between Gould and Steve Tudgay, with the Mail reporter now banned from the Hawthorns. The sledgehammer tactic was self-defeating as the football club had neither their own publicity channels, nor any skilled practitioners to operate one. The horrendously expensive and poorly operated

Clubcall certainly didn't count (a daily three-minute recorded telephone message at premium rates where everyone spoke soooo slowly) The dispute distracted from the job in hand, and supporters picked sides, depending on their point of view. Gould's insistence on the club bringing in Tim Exeter, an athletics coach, and psychologist Ian Edwards, largely passed unnoticed. In this era, such sophisticated assistance was highly unusual. Perhaps 'low-key' was best. Some supporters would invariably enquire whether the psychologist was employed for Gould.

In fairness, the Boss did give local talent a genuine chance. Young Stewart Bowen had a run of six matches (albeit predictably out of position) which included a sweet left foot volleyed goal against Peterborough. He made an impact elsewhere as Gary Strodder confirmed. *"Bowie is a genuine character on and off the pitch. He is a bundle of energy and the butt of all the jokes."* Comic references to stepladders featured regularly for five foot three Stewart. It was never quite clear when the squad were laughing with Bowen or at him. Stewart was raised in Greets Green, West Bromwich, so it's hard to imagine anyone more deserving of the title "local." There was always something a bit different about him. Other teenagers were warned off Stewart, though his charisma always saw him through. As he admitted himself: *"My schooldays didn't go too well to say the least."* By 19, he was already a Dad, a property owner, the proprietor of a TV and Video shop, and had a very active side line in sportswear. I had a Bowen tracksuit in my wardrobe for many years. Stewart was clear that if he didn't make it as a footballer, he'd *"turn into an Arthur Daley character – a wheeler dealer."* He was true to his word and has since built a reputation as an astute businessman across West Bromwich. Like Robbie Di Matteo, Stewart part owns an Italian restaurant.

The day of the Tigers match had another feature. The Football Supporters Association (FSA) worked with Grorty Dick fanzine on a petition against proposals for the Super League (later the Premier League). The spectacular success of the ID card petition three years earlier made the Hawthorns, and its radicalised inhabitants, an obvious place to start the supporter fightback. Signature collectors were stationed outside every turnstile block expecting brisk business. But they were disappointed. Around 1,500 signatures were amassed, a respectable number, but only about 15% of the total garnered against ID cards. The comparative apathy disheartened the campaigners and the exercise was not repeated elsewhere. How far the campaign might have got if Baggie people had demonstrated solid opposition is open to question.

The game at Preston was switched to midweek on Police advice; in other words, they couldn't cope with us and a Party Conference in Blackpool on the same Saturday. Albion suffered the same fate as most visitors who were unfamiliar with the vagaries of the hard, unyielding astroturf surface, and were defeated comfortably. The players suffered skin burns for their trouble. Gould's tactic of launching long balls during gale force winds didn't seem the best way of combating the conditions.

Still the Gould v Tudgay spat continued. Two pages of the programme for the Shrewsbury game was given over to the club's side. The piece was well-intentioned, but in its eagerness to build a comprehensive case included numerous minute details that were impossible to verify and frankly, who cared, really? The truth, as usual, probably lay somewhere in the middle. Gould introduced a simple policy for his players when dealing with the press *"don't tell them things and answer with great care anything they ask."*

On paper, the trip to second in the table Brentford looked a little daunting. The Bees could boast six straight wins. But weren't we the famous West Bromwich Albion? Over 3,000 supporters were lured by yet another new ground and the prospect of a pub on every corner. The long line of coaches parked in this quiet part of West London made for an impressive sight.

Paul Mason, then a stalwart of WBA Supporters Club, London Branch was trying to flog the branch fanzine 'Almost a Chant' without much success. *"Nobody's buying!"* he wailed repeatedly. Sales picked up when the Grorty Dick team leant their vocal backing, to the annoyance of one bloke in the nearby flats who'd been on night shift.

Albion played attractively, keeping the ball on the ground, and standing up to the agricultural tackling of the Londoners. None played better than the regularly lampooned Kwame Ampadu who gave the stripes the lead with a header.

The Bees equalised from a free kick with ten minutes remaining. Fanatical Baggie Chris Hartle, standing next to me, said *"we'll win this 2-1"*. Predictions from supporters are ten-a-penny, but his words were uttered with such conviction, and I believed. Even as the remaining sands of time ebbed away and in the face of noisy Brentford bellowing *"We are top of the League."* But Brentford weren't paying enough attention to Don Goodman, whose bold lob won the day. It was his fifth goal in five League matches.

"We Are Top of the League" we bellowed joyously in what was one of the most satisfying moments of the whole season. Chris Hartle's prediction was spot on, and that evening we believed that maybe, just maybe, Albion did have a team worthy of their traditions. But unbeknown to us, Goodman had already asked for a move.

Next up were the Bluenoses. Their shared acute anxiety to escape upwards led to a full house of 26,000, of which City were given 8,500 tickets (95% of their average gate) and they still moaned that wasn't enough. Their hooligan element bought tickets for the home terrace which inevitably led to Brummies fighting in the Brummie. Meanwhile, hidden within the Smethwick End masses, some Bluenoses let off fireworks, regardless of consequences. *"Please stop – you are injuring your own supporters"* was the urgent plea over the PA system, quickly followed by the pointed: *"You're so thick, you're unbelievable"* from the Brummie Road. Top of the League Albion, with Don Goodman in form, fancied their chances but a combination of missed chances and Paul Mardon's comprehensive marking job on our leading striker led to City pinching a 1-0 victory. Gould lost much credibility that afternoon.

Trying to get his mojo back, the Boss again tinkered with the line-up. He selected two youngsters – Bowen and Pritchard – in his midfield, an idea that even he admitted later wasn't very bright. As a consequence, Albion were outplayed at home by relegation-threatened Bury, who featured one Dean Kiely in goal. The team were booed off at half time, the choice of substitutes also got the bird and, despite Robson scrambling a late equaliser, the whole team were barracked again at the end. The natives were becoming increasingly restless. The attendance was badly affected by a clash with the Rugby Union World Cup Final. Among the absentees was Kelvin Whittaker, who had the excuse that he was getting married that afternoon. However, he'd still insisted on turning out for the Supporters football team that morning.

The pair of poor results were hardly an incentive to venture to one of the country's most obscure football locations, the Vic in Hartlepool, on Bonfire Night. Baggies followers were sated by new grounds by then, and less than 500 headed North. With 'Pools obliged to demolish their main stand due to wet rot, there was no protection from the biting wind and mist coming off the nearby North Sea. Around 2,800 shivering souls dressed like polar explorers endured, but their sacrifice was largely in vain. Strodder and Burgess defended stoutly to ensure a goalless draw. Some of the teeth-chattering Baggie followers took out their frustration on the latest boo-boy – Tony Ford. The midfielder had just admitted: *"his heart wasn't in it"* which sounded fishy. Indeed, he was shortly to be shipped off to Grimsby in exchange for real money. In its own way, the evening lived down to the worst stereotypes of the Division with Portakabins for the players and fairy rings (toadstool spores) in the turf.

Dean Walton was one of the 475 determined Baggies. *"This was the first time, in all my years of watching the Albion, that I actually questioned my own sanity. I had never been to Hartlepool, so I guess I just had to be there. I was working in Milton Keynes so endured a 4 hour drive to get there, only to stand on a freezing cold open terrace with the wind whistling in from the sea. The game was atrocious with 0-0 written all over it, I was soaking wet, freezing cold and knew full well that I had a mammoth drive back to MK afterwards. I stood there near the end of the game thinking "what the f**k am I doing here?"*

A warming whisky or two was essential to face the road home. North-East based Baggie Dawn Clennett and her Poolie-loving partner Andy hosted a disparate and desperate motley crew of Baggies in a warm local pub. And once again, we rebuilt our collective resilience.

After three grim matches, a 2-1 win at Reading surprised everyone. Goodman scored the opener, his first goal in four games, which was a fair reflection on a series of subdued performances. The Leeds-born striker was clear that he wanted out of the Division. Albion supporters also wanted out, but we didn't have an easy exit. Goodman won 8 dozen cans of beer from Reading sponsors Courage as Man of the Match which made for a very lively trip home for the team. Elm Park imposed a smoking ban in their old wooden main stand. At the time, this was considered a dreadful imposition upon the numerous smokers among our ranks. The toilets at half time were overflowing with pale-faced twitching supporters puffing furiously.

A First Round FA Cup draw against Non-League Marlow brought back unpleasant memories. The manager *"sensed a feeling of tension or even fear from the Halfords Lane tartan rug brigade."* By the time Marlow's defence had crumbled, Gould's attention was more focussed on arguing with a fan behind him. It was another indication of the pressure he was under. Marlow were no Woking and were buried 6-0. Don Goodman was to later regret turning out in this fixture Marlow was the first of three consecutive visitors to the Hawthorns. The others were far tougher encounters against fellow promotion hopefuls Huddersfield (beaten 2-1), and Stoke (drew 2-2). Both games showed how physically resilient Albion could be.

John Silk was proved right. The average gate was indeed up 1,500 on the previous season, though it wasn't enough to make a significant dent in WBA's overdraft. There was one obvious solution. Goodman wanted out, and Albion's bankers weren't prepared to wait for their thirty pieces of silver. News that he wanted out leaked before the draw with the potty Potters and he was predictably jeered. Albion supporters were now skilled barrackers.

As the gallant 350 fought their way up the congested A46 for a meaningless but novel Autoglass match at Lincoln, Albion's main striker was also heading North, but his trip to Sunderland was one-way. He'd signed for the Mackems for £900,000. Although a fine cameo role by Gary Robson gave the Baggies a 2-1 win over modest opposition, the question that night everyone was asking – who will score our goals? No, it felt bigger than that – "WHO WILL SCORE OUR GOALS?" Understandably, Bobby Gould felt like a limping man who'd lost his crutch.

Gould was struggling to retain his equilibrium. I was summoned into the manager's room in Halfords Lane. Apparently, my wife's powerful fanzine selling exhortations outside his office were distracting key talks with parents over signing their "little Johnny". The reasoning made little sense, putting aside the question that if he had a problem with my wife, why he couldn't just talk to her. With only 20 minutes to kick-off, why wasn't he with the team? "*I won't be there for another ten minutes*" explained Gould. He looked generally ill-at-ease during our meeting. To relieve Gould's tensions, the sales team were temporarily re-positioned. For one game only. As if to prove that someone still loved him, Wimbledon Chairman Sam Hamman gave him a new BMW as recognition for his efforts with the Dons. The present was far from the spontaneous gesture as it was portrayed. Gould had apparently been nagging him for a parting gift for years. As you do.

A seven-match unbeaten run had built belief, but the Goodman sale terminated all that. *"Once again, the flame of optimism has been snuffed out as soon as it flickers into life"* lamented Devon-based Baggie Simon Bywater. Five nights later, in a live FA Cup Second Round fixture at Leyton Orient, the whole country could see the new toothless Albion. The Baggies dominated virtually the whole match, but only had Williams' header to show for their efforts. The Londoners scrambled goals in the 1st and the 88th minute to steal the tie. The shock of elimination before the Third Round numbed the shivering Albion contingent on another cold and very open terrace. Visiting supporters couldn't be trusted with a roof. The Sky studio was in a Portakabin-on-stilts situated over the away terrace, Better known these days for his opinion about female officials, Richard Keys was then famed for his hairy hands and arms. This prompted a large number of Baggies fans to jump up and down mimicking orang-utans in the hope of catching his eye!

The struggle continued. The 1-1 draw at Bradford City was chiefly memorable for Daryl Burgess throwing up during the warm-up. This was followed by a 3-1 win over Darlington, who included a youthful pert-bottomed Sean Gregan. Neither result quite satisfied supporters. *"WBA are effluent rather than affluent following the sale of Goodman"* was a splendid one-liner coined by fan David Norman. He added: *"All we seem to do is loft the high ball up the centre of the pitch, hoping for a lucky defensive error or a favourable touch from Williams to produce an opportunity."*

In this year of virgin grounds and no electronic aids, finding Third Division venues was not always easy. Founder member of Sutton Branch WBASC, Steve Davies, found Springfield Park in Wigan particularly elusive. Then he spotted director Clive Stapleton's highly distinctive car. Surely a club director would know the right way? So scarves fluttering, he tucked in behind him. Within seconds, another car load of supporters joined them. Then another .. and another. The unsuspecting

Clive Stapleton was quickly leading a ten-car convoy. He drove on boldly towards a set of towering floodlights and the ground came into view.. Central Park, home of Wigan RLFC. Oh whoops. A certain fanzine editor made notes about club directors being uncertain about future direction... In fairness, Clive wasn't the only reluctant guide ending up at the wrong ground followed by a gaggle of cars, were they Thomas Lewin?

Steve, Clive and the rest were just a tiny part of the 2,500 visitors in Wigan, an impressive attempt to bring civilisation to such an ancient settlement. Springfield Park had an official limit of 11,000 (with room for double that) but even with the hefty boost of the Baggies support, the attendance barely topped 5,000. The majority of visitors stood on either the few steps of crescent shaped terrace behind one goal or the steep muddy grass bank above the terrace. The grass gave some kind of view over the ridiculous "safety" fence but it wasn't easy to maintain your balance. Such as flu victim Kevin Elcock who was already having a rotten day. He felt the need to keep shuffling his feet to ease his discomfort. After an hour or so, he'd completely worn away the grass so moved to another spot. Within minutes, his mate slipped on the newly built patch, cursing horribly.

The tiny toilets were at the top of said muddy banks and after copious use, the drains gave up the unequal struggle and sewage oozed down the bank. My niece was one of many inadvertently taking the quick way down the incline. Another unfortunate wearing a gorgeous sheepskin coat needed a visit to the dry cleaners after his tumble. Cumbrian based Baggie John Keogh was unable to forget: *"waiting in a queue outside the bogs watching a flowing stream of urine pouring out of the entrance."* Another Albionite complained bitterly that his one day old suede shoes were ruined. What would Lord Justice Taylor make of this arrangement? When challenged later, Athletic's Safety Officer insisted the local authority were happy with the arrangements. Frankly, they were taking the pee.

The effort made by the Black Country hordes for a noon kick-off (another Police imposition) went largely unrewarded. On a very cold day, the two teams took turns to thump howitzers down the pitch. Goodman-less Albion scraped a 1-0 win with a Shakespeare penalty (see below). The three points were welcome but the fayre was just so grim ...The Baggies were third, unbeaten in 8 League matches and had kept the bank manager happy. But few bar the club manager were content.

Two days later came another novelty fixture – a visit to St James' Park. Yes, the famous one in Devon. The Grecians effortlessly slipped into their wind-up mode (had they rehearsed?). They took particular delight in chanting: *"you're not famous any more"* and to be frank, it did get to us all. Both goals in a grind of a 1-1 draw were penalties. City's, painfully, came just two minutes from time. Our hitherto-classy loanee Frank Sinclair allegedly head butted referee Paul Alcock and received a 9 match ban. Many observers saw only an accidental collision which Alcock exaggerated. Six years later, a push by Di Canio had the same official staggering around again like a ham actor. Once his suspension was confirmed, Sinclair's long ban abruptly ended his Albion days

Still, the hard-fought point was enough to put WBA in top spot, with the Division's best away record. Author Richard Brentnall was unimpressed by mere facts: *"Albion use statistics rather like a drunken man uses a lamp-post: not so much for illumination as support."* His simile was well chosen as his mates swore that Ritchie's alcoholic consumption that weekend had been prodigious (and produced the photographs to prove it), yet his written report was even more lucid than normal.

Albion's fortunes abruptly nose-dived, just as everyone predicted they would *sans Goodman*. Fulham travelled to the Hawthorns on New Year's Day, and went home with three points. In truth, there was little wrong with the Baggies' attacking endeavours in the 2-3 setback, but there was everything wrong with supporters' mood swings and confidence levels. *"Where's the money gone?"* had its first airing. Donkey noises were directed at Paul Williams, who privately admitted to being shocked by the abuse bellowed at him. "Bruiser" Naylor and Darren Rogers were also targeted.

Seven days after the previous trip to Devon, fixture planners sent us back again for a League match at Plainmoor. As this was Third Round Day, several confused journalists thought the fixture was a Cup match and thus we were knocked out for a second time. There was a backhanded compliment in there somewhere. The Third Round and WBA obviously go together.

Bombing down the M5, I'd almost reached Torquay when I was flagged down by desperate Albion supporters on the hard shoulder whose minibus had broken down. Trying to be a caring, sharing fanzine editor, I squeezed two of the group onto the back seat, where Martin Lewis forcibly introduced himself. Over the decades, Potteries-based Martin has built a reputation as being rather talkative. Most regulars know to sidle away when Martin launched into his favourite anecdotes, but these hapless victims were *"fresh meat for the grinder."* He talked non-stop for the 30 minutes required to reach Plainmoor, his voice becoming steadily shriller. Without waiting for the car to come to a complete standstill, the pair already had the door open. *"Do you need a lift back?"* I called to their backs as they bolted up the road....

Due to injuries, Albion started with an odd-looking back three of Roberts, Sinclair and Rogers, none of whom had a future at the club.

In a grim battle between two nervous teams, Torquay won 1-0, with a late Justin Fashanu goal. The Fash remains to this day, the only professional footballer to admit publicly to being gay. He was in imperious form, literally unabashed by Roberts' attempt to subdue him. Neither was he deterred by the gay taunts from the away terrace. During this era, such homophobic taunts were rarely challenged. Sadly, Justin was to take his own life seven years later.

This was another angry afternoon for our support. The repeated *"What a load of rubbish"* referred equally to both the team performance, and the dreadful state of the ground. Some of our number waved flags calling for John Silk to resign. It didn't help our mood that Torquay seemed hell-bent on packing people inside regardless of whether they could actually see or not. Some seats were badly restricted views but United try to take the money anyway. At least one supporter marooned behind a pillar in the seats, later successfully claimed and secured a full refund. Standing on the six steps of terrace (uncovered – naturally) behind the goal was a better bet than the cramped, dirty seats. Bizarrely, there was so much flat land behind this bump of concrete that a ball was produced from somewhere and a 20+ a side kickabout filled the pre-kick off minutes.

Once again, local Police were making a big issue out of our visit. The local Torquay Herald Express reported "*Torquay police hailed as a success their operation to ensure the clash between Torquay United and West Bromwich Albion passed peacefully.*" Why wouldn't it? We had no axe to grind with Torquay. We'd never played them in a League match before, and thanks to their tiny ground, only had 800 supporters. Our beef was with our own. Police escorted our manager off the pitch, and then gave him an escort out of town. Cynics considered an escort an excellent idea, providing it was one way. Not all shared these views and heated arguments broke out between the Gould-haters and those who pointed out that not everything could be laid at his door. Torquay was another contender for lowest moment of the season.

With hindsight, it's intriguing to highlight the strong Albion connections at Torquay. As well as ex-Baggies Colcombe and Dobbins in the Gulls team, Paul Holmes lined up at full-back while among their apprentices was one Darren Moore.

During this month, Gary Bannister offered numerous frank comments at a Supporters Club meeting in Evesham. His observations never reached a wide audience; however, Gould's response was not to admonish the player but rather to ban all players from all supporters' functions. One of the most endearing features of this era was the accessibility to players. Their willingness to travel to interact with fans was almost taken for granted during a period when the "us" and "them" divide was so much narrower than it is today. Gould's banning order was dreadful PR and directly impacted on the WBA Supporters Club, normally a very conservative and supportive bunch. Now the manager had even got their backs up.

Bannister, the free-speech striker, had gone 11 months without a goal, which partly explained why he let his frustrations rip in Evesham. His desert-like drought finally ended a week later with two goals in a comfortable 4-0 victory over Bournemouth. Yet supporters were only mildly pleased, howling "*Sack the Board.*" We were collectively in a bad place where not even victories could no longer be fully enjoyed.

Media comments from followers of other clubs described WBA fans as "paranoid" and in "near panic." They didn't or couldn't understand our concerns.

This angst was reflected in a full page of Board bashing letters in the Argus. Most were based around a simplistic logic that "*Albion cannot be in debt because they have the biggest gates in the Division.*" The scribes couldn't or wouldn't grasp that a club with 32 professionals in the Third Division, unable to sell any of them because of their high wages, had to go cap in hand to the bank. Furthermore, if Albion were to gain promotion, they would have to quickly find sufficient funds from somewhere to convert their terracing into seats. The Baggies, in reality, were in a grim financial state. But even though some fans couldn't grasp basic finance, both the letter writing and the chanting showed a burning hunger for change.

The manager-reporter divide was increasingly tedious, yet the protagonists continued to hammer away. "*What didn't help was the Birmingham Evening Mail*" moaned Gould. "*They were against me and I found myself getting attacked on a daily basis. The relationship between the club and the local press is always very important. But they were trying to run West Brom and wouldn't let me run it.*"

Any hopes of a Wembley trip in the Mickey Mouse Cup were abruptly ended at home by Exeter. The few supporters who travelled with the Grecians reminded us again that we "*weren't famous any more.*" Teeth-gnashing all round.

These were strange, difficult times. Arriving early morning for their match with their Orient counterparts, the WBA Supporters football team (the Strollers) were taken aback to find Brisbane Road unlocked and deserted. The temptation to go in and wander around was too great to resist, so too the temptation to write something on the blackboard in the Albion dressing room. Oh, there was so much debate among the amateur footballers but in the end, all that was left was a best wishes message.

The big game ended in a draw. Pressed into service as a striker, Gary Robson missed two great chances, which again highlighted the need for Albion to sign a forward. Predictably, the message was made clear from the away terracing. Power to the people!

Swansea at home was next. If Albion supporters were "paranoid" and "in near panic" beforehand, then it was well nigh impossible to describe the mood after this latest candidate for club all-time low-point. Two goals from Graham Roberts (one a spectacular effort) gave the Baggies a comfortable lead, surely sufficient to see out the rest of the match, even though Cradley-born John Williams was frightening us with his pace. Wrong! Assisted by dismal, nervous defending, notably from Naylor in goal, City's substitute Steve Thornber scored a hat-trick in the last 12 minutes to turn victory into defeat.

The afternoon was summed up by Leon Hickman in the Evening Mail. *"In the first half I counted 23 passes struck out of blind hope, 18 finding Swansea players, second half 11 misses out of 18. The only route open to Division Two is by way of biff-bang football, so I'm afraid fans will have to endure it. I hope I never grow to like it though.*

With heavy echoes of Woking, the Police concentrated on "protecting" the away supporters, with around 60 officers surrounding the Welshmen, who, naturally, were irritated that they'd been treated like criminals.

After briefly invading the pitch, around 500 Baggies supporters decided they weren't leaving without answers. *"Where's the money gone?"* they bellowed repeatedly, interspersed by *"Silk out."* An hour later, they were still defiantly gathered on the Brummie, resisting all attempts at dispersal. To his utmost credit, Bobby Gould volunteered to address the maddened crowd face-to-face, and answer any questions put to him. *"I would be willing to stay with those fans all night..."* he explained via the Albion News. No manager before or since has made such a bold fan-friendly move.

The impromptu meeting, and the manager's charm, calmed everyone down, especially as he promised a striker would be signed by the end of the week. Steve Sant was one of the protestors. He explained: *"the anger wasn't aimed at Gould personally or even the players, but was an outburst of frustration which had built up over the last decade or so."* The club attempted a PR initiative but without ammunition or skills to do the job properly, encouraged supporters to send in questions. I called their bluff and hand-delivered twenty-four of them. The Chairman told me I was being *"negative"* but did agree to what turned out to be a two-hour interview for the fanzine. Most of the questions were answered after barriers were originally put up leading me to ponder who was really being negative.

It's now basic supporter knowledge that Bob Taylor was the striker who the manager had promised. Such was the all-encompassing downbeat mood that not everyone welcomed his arrival. *"No player with any sense is going to sign for a Third Division club unless they are Fourth Division or Non-League"* sternly warned Stourbridge-based Baggie David Vine. In addition to "No-sense" Bob Taylor, the Baggies coincidentally did indeed make a signing from a Fourth Division side. Goalkeeper Jonathan Gould couldn't get out of Halifax quick enough to sign for the Baggies. Gould Junior was a decent keeper and man, and had his name been Smith then his later Scottish international caps could have been earned in an Albion shirt. But he was the manager's son and therefore permanently tarnished. He was to leave West Brom later without making a single first team appearance. Meanwhile, with no trust in the Board, some supporters continued to lash out wildly for quick fixes such as laughably suggesting approaching Eric Clapton to become an investor. The new arrivals signed up just before a trio of heavyweight matches against promotion rivals – Brentford, Birmingham

City and Stoke City. To prepare, Gould's men endured another three days at an army barracks, at a time when other local clubs were sending their players abroad. Such activities are always measured against results, thus Albion's 2-0 defeat of leaders Brentford made the Jalalabad excursion look worthy.

Unlike WBA's previous expensive striker signing, Bob Taylor only needed one early chance to score his first goal. After that, fans were firmly behind both him and the team, as they held off the Londoners' muscular effort with some ease.

When his goal was followed by two more at St Andrews in a 3-0 demolition of the 'Noses, supporters moods shifted from one extreme to the other. We were top of the League again, with a real goalscorer and what seemed like an effective side at last. Graham Roberts, now sitting in midfield, really looked the part. Perhaps the old pro could smell another chance to secure the managers' job.

The Birmingham victory felt huge. In front of 27,000, Blues had a player sent off early quickly followed by Gary Robson's spectacular opener. Bob's diving header (a classic Taylor 'right time, right place' gamble) to double the advantage started a revolt. Blues supporters surged up and down their huge terraces, battling with Police. The aggression matched that on the pitch.

In desperation, the Blues manager did a pre-Warnock, bringing on the large, aggressive John Gayle apparently just to damage opposition players. He gave Darren Bradley a couple of fearful whacks before the old warhorse Graham Roberts had a "word", and Gayle was "calmed down." That was more than could be said for the Blues followers who were out for Albion blood after the match, rampaging along Garrison Lane. It was a quite naked display of hooliganism and rare for the period. The street was so grim already that it was well-nigh impossible to cause any damage to property but mounted Police were thankfully on hand to protect our people.

Once we were safely out of the area, there was much cause for celebration. According to a later supporter survey, all over the Black Country that night, there were men and women drinking themselves silly on the strength of the derby win.

Now we believed. A 4,500 strong Albion army travelled North to support the League Leaders at the Victoria Ground, Stoke. Supporters queued impatiently outside turnstiles under heavy rain, with many missing the kick-off as the potty Potters were swamped. In the chaos, even people with tickets were turned away. Of those that got in, many were squeezed into small high-fenced terrace pens with limited shelter from the elements. The "Vic" was more miserable than usual.

Among our ranks was police officer Dawn Astle. She could have been on duty that night, collecting £60 overtime (then a sum sufficient to cover a dozen home matches) in exchange for marshalling chattering Stokies, but preferred to be with her own. Dawn was probably the only Staffs copper not on duty that night. The operation even extended to Police motorcyclists blocking off every M6 exit right down to Junction11 to ensure that our supporters really were going home. Perhaps they'd mistaken us for IRA terrorists.

As usual, Stoke had muscle and purpose, plus bloody noisy supporters and won 1-0 in the familiar dull affair. Bannister had a glorious late chance to grab a point but missed. It was a seminal moment. A single point would have maintained our momentum and morale but defeat raised the doubt and encouraged the doubters again. We didn't know then, but our last false dawn had come and gone. There were more memorable matches and moments to come, but nearly all of them for the wrong reasons.

In the latest WBA PR *faux pas*, the Supporters Club publication, Fingerpost, was banned from selling inside the ground for criticising the Board. The editors had been naive, if not stupid in their editing, but there were more mature ways to resolve differences all round at such a tense time. Strained relations were much in evidence at the Hawthorns days later when a clearly exasperated Gould threw the ball forcibly at his captain, Craig Shakespeare, during a break in play. It was the only lasting memory of an otherwise dull 1-1 draw against Bradford City.

With Albion still in third place, sufficient belief remained for 2,000 people to traipse down to Dean Court. It was Bradford all over again, but worse. The team humped the ball forward, and the powerful Cherries back division slung it back again. The home side scored with their first shot, and the well supported visitors had no coherent answer. Such was the dark mood that Trigger Taylor's last-minute consolation in a 2-1 defeat didn't even raise a cheer. It was a limp showing; one which any professional knew was unacceptable. However, Gould came up with a new motivational tactic; *"to achieve a sense of pride."* He'd overheard a small knot of supporters raging outside the dressing room, and invited one of them, Mick Caldicott, to share his thoughts with the players. Still a familiar face today, Mick was no diplomat and was single-minded enough to do the manager's bidding. During his tirade, the manager lost whatever was left of his credibility. Mick is of generous proportions and can no doubt handle himself so it's interesting to speculate as to whether the shell shocked players would have been quite so passive with a smaller fan. According to quotes attributed to Mick: *"they sat and took my criticism. I think they knew I was a genuine supporter who was upset"* although he later complained he'd been misquoted, with some justification. The phrases didn't really remotely Mick-like neither did his apparent exercise in semantics: *"I was not yelling abuse outside the dressing room. We were giving the players a hard time, that's all."* Reporters wanted words to fit their angle and basically made them up. It was commonplace then.

Perhaps it was fortunate Albion didn't have a PR person, as the temptation for him or her to seek a darkened room and a loaded revolver would have been very strong. Once again, one of the League's founder members was a national figure of fun, and now Gould had no-one willing to defend his corner. Jeff Astle was blunt: *"it seems to me that the manager is trying to make mugs out of the players."* The players agreed but felt unable to air their grievances in public though years later Bernie McNally admitted to me: *"I didn't play but I was listening to it on the radio and I thought "you've lost the lads now" because if you do something like that, you get a players revolt. I think with hindsight he knew he'd done the wrong thing. Even the minority of players who were still behind him, had to hold their hands up then and say "well actually, he was*

out of order doing that."
In theory, the promotion race continued, so a week later, desperate Albion lined up against even more desperate Torquay. The doomed Gulls hadn't won away all season but now had a new manager to impress. Presumably, the new gaffer was a part-time cage wrestler, which is why his yellow-shirted men kicked anything that moved. Worse, referee Edward Parker lost control which effectively left the Devonians to carry on kicking.

Albion may not have been a very good team but they were *our* not very good team. We would not stand silently and watch them being bullied. Vitriol poured down upon Parker from all sides. He belatedly produced a flurry of yellow cards but this didn't calm the aggression.

The Baggies finally found a way through the visitors' defence late in the game. The scorer was YTS trainee Roy Hunter, yet another young talent given an opportunity. Our late winner felt like a glorious triumph for fair play but Torquay players became even wilder. Finally, referee Parker sent off three players, Bradley and two of the visitors including Fashanu. "Fash" knew his career was on borrowed time and this was manifested in a series of desperate lunges. This cameo felt more like a brutal Cup match than a League game.

The 1-0 win over the soon-to-be-Fourth-Division Torquay was sufficient to maintain Albion's third spot and promotion, at least to outsiders, remained realistic. For those closer to the action, "promotion drive" resembled a half-hearted unsteady lurch. There was simply no harmony between players, management, supporters, local press and the Board.

This state of affairs wasn't unique to the Hawthorns. In the frozen wastelands of the North-East, Newcastle United decided Ossie Ardiles was no longer motivating the players and sacked him. The Argentinean had lasted less than a year in the role, so the validity was dubious, but the sacking was certainly a decisive statement. The latest entrant to the 'For Hire' ranks prompted a few wistful sighs and comments among the Woodman pub regulars before the home match against Leyton Orient.

Their wistfulness became strident as the East Londoners

accepted all three of their early chances, and then successfully defended their lead. Criticism was both quick and savage. *"We want six"* was the ironic cry, followed by the familiar *"Silk Out."* The Brummie Road regulars morphed into a raging mob, figuratively striking out blindly in all directions. Much was made of Gould changing his team line-up again with no-one wanting to hear that squad rotation was sensible because of a heavy period of games. Despite being a night game, there was another determined sit-in protest. This time, Gould stayed in the dressing room.

A desperately dull Friday night goalless draw at Swansea followed. It was enlivened only by use of the comically awful "facilities" – namely an under-liquid Ladies, and a Gents which consisted of a slight dent in a concrete surface. "Catering" was supplied through a small gap in a huge metal fence.

Entertainment was provided by a decent number of Cardiff supporters who joined us in the away end. They were disappointed that WBA couldn't beat the White Taffs but happily did the "Ayatollah." They even encouraged bemused Black Country folk to join in. (*"Do the Ayatollah"* is a City trademark dating back to 1990 and involves holding both hands flat pointing towards each other raised above your head and repeatedly moving them up and down in a patting motion).

Any entertainment, even the bizarre emulation of excitable Islamic clerics, was welcome.

An away game was followed by a home match - quite common during this era. Feelings were confused for the first-ever visit by Hartlepool. Some fans dreamed of promotion, citing the indifferent form of rivals, while others wished for defeat and another 'Bash Gould' night; with the rest somewhere in the middle. Most simply couldn't bear the thought of losing to one of the country's least successful professional clubs. In truth, the Poolies' image of permanently staving off Non-League football was terribly dated, but the perception lingered.

Prior to kick-off, I entertained Andy, a Pools supporter who we'd met at the Vic. Andy was as aware of the "mismatch" as we were, but laughed off any suggestion that United might catch Albion at the right time.

Pools were gifted a penalty after just four minutes. After scoring, the visitors dominated. *"Losing at home to Hartlepool was not a scenario they had spent much of their lives contemplating"* observed one of the 'Pools fan sites. Being forced to consider this possibility was too much. Some fans left at half time, including Bob Smith from Kingswinford moaning *"I can't watch any more of this."* Gould made changes (again) introducing both substitutes at half time but then Graham Roberts hobbled off, so the Baggies were reduced to ten men. In truth, the home side were now on top, but their efforts met only with scorn. Here was another worthy candidate for the club's lowest point in their history. Football historian Steve Carr is clear that this was his personal nadir of the season, though not quite the worst-ever point of his Albion supporting life which will forever be rooted in the grim Ron Saunders era.

Significantly, on this night there was a new unified target for abuse – Bobby Gould. *"We want Gouldy out..."* a blunt comment which ratcheted up further when the North Eastern club found the net again. There were some cries for the doyen of passing football, Pancho Pearson, to be his replacement. As Stuart himself admitted later *"It was bloody uncomfortable sitting in the dug-out against Hartlepool and the fans chanting*

my name and *"Gould Out when I was sat next to him."*
Our players argued that merely because Williams put three defenders in the Hartlepool net with the ball, there was no reason to disallow the goal. While the debate continued, United broke quickly and scored their second. The final score of 1-2, Albion's fifth home League defeat, led to another 50 minute post-match protest. Tempers flared as Police and stewards moved in to forcibly move the demonstrators outside the ground. Gould, caught in a wistful mood, confessed *"Perhaps if I could go back to Christmas, I might have taken another direction."* Too late.

It was difficult to imagine how the manager could make himself any less popular, but Gould quickly found a way within 48 hours. On his insistence, Stuart Pearson was suspended and subsequently sacked a fortnight later.

The precise reason for this action has never been made clear. At the time, Gould would only say that Pearson hadn't supported him. Twenty years later, his biography offered only the enigmatic: *"what I should have done was ask Pearson to leave earlier than I did because it didn't work between us."*
This angle was confirmed by young Stewart Bowen: *"Gould and Pearson never hit it off with each other. There was always tension."*
Supporter Michael Corfield had no doubts. *"Pearson banned me from watching training after my mates and I told Gould that the players were just messing about in training. I'd been there, and seen the players just kicking balls anywhere with Pearson just laughing. The final straw came when Pancho picked on an OAP. I had an altercation with him until Graham Roberts held me back and advised me to "leave it.""* At the time, Albion trained on Halfords Lane and, with a delicious irony, there was a Circus on the car park.

But why was Pearson sacked that particular week, other than as a crude reaction to the Brummie Road chants? Chairman John Silk wouldn't share the official reason with me, either on the record or off it. The timing of the suspension brought with it an implication that Pearson was somehow responsible for the team's poor form. Pearson himself maintained a dignified silence for several months before he could contain himself no longer: *"I should have walked before the manager did a number on me. The writing was on the wall and I should have spotted it. I was being ignored and left out of things, not even coaching the first team. People were led to believe I stabbed Gould in the back. To this day, I have never been told why I was first suspended and then sacked."*

With delicious irony, supporters had their first chance to give their verdict from the fenced Cemetery End in Bury, with the valuable boost of a roof and wooden floor for the travelling 1,500 or so. *"Pearson's Blue and White Army..."* was first aired before kick-off, and regularly repeated during the game, with a sustained chorus during the drab second half. Pancho Pearson was perceived as the last vestige of passing football, the last objector to Gould's excesses and also because "my enemy's enemy is my friend."

The Lancastrians scored and Bob Taylor equalised. Both goals came within the first eight minutes and that was all the excitement. The rest of the match saw the visitors on top, but completely unable to muster any fluency. A small group tried a counter-chant of *"Gould's Barmy Army"* but the attempts just created fissures in the ranks. Gigg Lane was a sad, angry place to be with supporters raging at each other, the dugout and the players. And yet despite the divisions, fan power made a statement. Albion folk made up half the gate.

The gnawing frustrations at Bury were carried over for the visit of Reading to the Hawthorns. *And such anger!* Gould, presumably unconsciously, stoked the fires once again, by switching the formation to 4-5-1. At this time, any club lining up with only one forward was deemed to be highly negative and not operating within the spirit of the game. Two more rookies, in the shape of Neil Cartwright and Carl Heggs, were blooded in a harsh environment.

The manager was booed when he emerged from the tunnel. He responded by shaking his fist at the Brummie Road. Whether this was to encourage or express his anger wasn't clear, but he was jeered again anyway, just to be sure. This set the tone. Every ground pass was cheered. Every aerial clearance was booed, and followed by choruses of *"We Want Football"*. Numerous anti-Gould chants followed and even Albion taking the lead didn't change the tone. *"We still hate you, Bobby Gould"* came the response.

By the break, WBA were two goals ahead, and comfortable but that was no longer enough. The negativity continued apace. The substitutes were barracked, particularly the increasingly forlorn Paul Williams. This was simply another desperate afternoon. The intensity of the barracking was so powerful that moderate supporters were appalled. Everyone was ranting irrationally at everyone else. In this scenario, John Silk's thoughts that: *"none of the Albion directors enjoy home games any more"* made sad sense. If you give supporters a winning team, and they're still unhappy, where do you go?

Ground director Trevor Summers went further. As usual. Not for the first time, he shot from the hip: *"Albion would be better off playing behind closed doors than in front of their own fans."* Mail reporter Tudgay couldn't believe his luck with that line. Such a barb was acceptable for a disinterested drinker to make in a local pub, but quite unacceptable from a club Director.

Once again, the absence of a PR professional had led to the bonfire being stacked a little higher with Gould as the Guy. Something had to be done to break this self-destructive cycle. With WBA in third place again, promotion could still be grabbed from the ashes. Feeling that supporters needed a new focus, I had a go at providing one.

I worked in partnership with the Last Train to Rolfe Street fanzine (the new vehicle for the editors of Fingerpost). I wrote a handbill while they arranged the printing. The leaflet asked for a mutual commitment from supporters to put their grievances with individuals to one side and simply back the team for the rest of the season. All sellers would distribute leaflets at two Saturday games to both customers and non-customers alike.

First up was Leeds Road and a meeting with fellow promotion hopefuls Huddersfield. Many hundreds of leaflets were given out. A few fans reacted strongly (one was sadly arrested for his antics of jostling one of the canvassers) but nearly all seemed willing to consider the idea.

The atmosphere inside the old barn of stadium was odd. There were no anti-Gould chants from the 2,500 following, but there was no real support either, more standing back and waiting to be entertained or appalled. One group did bellow abuse at Williams during the warm-up. The leaflet played a part, but so too did the all-round realisation that barracking a winning team the previous week was OTT.

The Yorkshiremen were in desperately poor form themselves so, in theory, the Baggies had the chance to attack Town and get their own season back on course. But Gould was going for safety with a defensive 4-5-1 line-up. Jeff Astle considered the formation was *"that of a frightened man. Fans came up to me before kick-off looking dazed."* Truth be told, our team were looking rather dazed ... and confused too. When Gary Strodder scored a spectacular own goal for Town's third, the anti-Gould feeling could be held back no more. The jeering was quite muted, but only because of a mass exodus from the away end, and the lack of a roof. Fine words in a leaflet cannot compensate for a performance so grim that the King admitted: *"it made me want to cry."* Most everyone knew how he felt. As Darren Bradley beavered increasingly frantically in Albion's midfield, he looked close to tears himself.

Four days later, Gould tried another of his now-infamous motivational stunts. Back in the day, he'd driven his Wimbledon team across London to an FA Cup Semi Final in a minibus. The Dons won that day so the same stunt was inflicted on a by-now thoroughly dejected Albion team, all the way to Stockport. The payoff for being cramped in a minibus with the manager at the wheel was another 3-0 defeat. The all-ticket Albion support was most unimpressed. One regular, a fully-turbaned elderly Sikh, and normally of quite dignified demeanour during games, exploded with complete and utter fury at the front of the away end, just before the final whistle. He wasn't alone.

Dean Walton: *"I just lost it. I climbed over the wall and walked around the pitch towards the dug-out (nobly my mate Silve followed but he was on crutches at the time). I just marched straight past the stewards and found myself face to face with Mr Gould. I said: "This is my club and you're destroying it. The mighty West Bromwich Albion are losing 3-0 to Stockport County, for fu**s sake."* I went on: *"Please resign now and give us a chance to go up"* Gould just looked at me in disbelief and told me to move out of the way. Then I was led away by some surprisingly sympathetic stewards."* Both Gould and Chairman John Silk had Police escorts after the match but as Silk himself pointed out: *"This was just a precaution. There was no lynch mob outside."*

A few diehards including Richard Brentnall, sought alcoholic refreshment in the town centre before setting off home in the early hours. Their final stop was a kebab house in an unremarkable back street. Richard takes up the story: "*we became aware of half a dozen kids lolling around in tracksuits, and stuffing their faces after what might, for all the world, have been a spot of ten-pin bowling or five-a-side. Just kids on an evening out, except that these harmless looking kids had just stuffed by three clear goals West Bromwich Albion. Good luck to them, I thought, and we all wished them so too, but it didn't half bring home the reality of our situation.*"

The Albion manager was now a marked man. Against Phil Neal's Bolton, abuse was howled at him every time he left the dugout. But after Albion lost loanee keeper Dibble (or *Dribble* as the Argus once unfortunately called him) and had to continue with a defender in goal, everyone pulled together to face the crisis. With their supporters firmly behind them, the Baggies recovered from a 2-1 deficit to draw. Pulling together for the good of the club was a point Gould had made repeatedly, but no-one was listening to him anymore. His latest observation was poignant. "*The supporters don't know me. If they were to spend some time with me behind the scenes, they might understand me a bit better and change their opinions.*" Refusing the numerous requests from Supporters Club branches was coming back to haunt him. Understandably, the players were feeling the strain. Bernie McNally confessed to: "*losing my love of the game completely. I hate training, the style of football.. everything. This season has been the worst of my life.*" Despite only being in his mid-twenties, he was considering retirement.

Draws against Peterborough, Chester and a defeat by Hull City followed in miserable succession. Not only had automatic promotion slipped away, so too did the play-offs. Still Gould lingered. Months later, Trevor Summers explained why: "*The disruption of a manager leaving when we still had a slight chance of promotion is a bad thing.*" Really? As opposed to the ongoing unrest due to not sacking the manager.

The embarrassment and the hurt were mounting. Gould agreed to appear at a Sports Forum hosted by George Gavin but then ducked it. Gavin had a room full of people and no guest. He improvised, asking supporters to question an empty chair, and then broadcast the outcome. Writing in his biography decades later, the Albion boss admitted: *"I became a coward and I hid. The worst example of that was running away from a George Gavin forum on the local radio. I chickened out and it was a huge mistake. It just gave the local media more to hit me with."* Possibly Gould had had some form of nervous breakdown by this point. It would explain much of his bizarre behaviour. If so, all the more reason for getting the manager out of the firing line. Perhaps the Board were happy to leave him in place as the whipping boy to deflect attention from their own efforts?

But at least the miserable season was finally reaching a conclusion. With 16 players out of contract in the summer, the Baggies had a chance to reshuffle their pack. But to do so effectively would require fresh leadership. Writing in the Argus, Glynis Wright adapted a famous quote: *"You have sat too long here for any good you have been doing. Depart I say and let us have done with you. In the name of God, go."* Many others used similar but less elegant words.

In their final Hawthorns fixture, Albion easily beat a disinterested Preston North End but, just like Reading, a mere win couldn't deflect attention away from the greater objective. *"Silk Out"* and *"Gould Out"* chants were incessant. The mood was already tense as news of Blues' promotion filtered through, and was unnecessarily racked up when Police tried to eject supporters waving an anti-Gould banner. Preston supporters earned significant applause when they joined in with *"Gould Out"*. Then, fights broke out between North End fans and the Police, with vocal Albion supporters barracking the Police. It is football, Jim, but not as we know it. No chance of relieving your stress at the Hawthorns, you'd end up leaving with more anxiety than when you arrived.

Gould received a tongue-lashing every time any part of his anatomy became visible in the dugout. According to his completely lost-the-plot programme notes, the fact that he'd had a happy childhood gave him armour against fate. That's alright then.

With WBA five points short of the play-offs with only two

games remaining, Gould might have been dismissed before Preston, thus relieving much angst all round. It was an open secret that he'd got the Coventry job lined up. Most supporters were already discussing who the next managerial mug would be. The name of Ardiles was most frequently mentioned, more in hope than expectation. As ex-defender Martyn Bennett noted; *"there is too much of a divide between the club and the supporters."* Club officials hung on grimly to power like a despotic African President in the face of overwhelming opposition.

The finale was 'Barmy Bobby's Beachwear Party' at Gay Meadow, Shrewsbury. Dean Walton and his chum Dubbsey had plugged the event for months. Although the game was all-ticket, the relegated Shrews wanted to swell their coffers and so 5,000 Albion supporters took advantage of their common sense approach. As well as 600 seats, we were given half of the terracing in this charming but tatty stadium, on the banks of the Severn. The mood was positive, ostensibly a celebration that the season was over at last, but with the underlying message that this day must be 'Goodbye to Gould'.

The whole area was swamped by people wearing various

ludicrous combinations of "beachwear". There were flags, thousands of balloons and beach balls. And a coffin. The media loved the coffin, and all subsequent references to the match invariably mentioned this wooden box or pictured it.
 But even during what he must have recognised as his swansong, Gould managed the unexpected. During a pre-match team walkabout in the town centre, the manager walked loud and proud, earning much admiration from Bob Taylor for his bravery (or cussedness?). The masses of Albion supporters that they passed were too startled to react. Then, as a piece-de-resistance, the team ran out in beachwear for their warm-up. It was a rare intelligent gesture, which was appreciated. As for the match, the Shropshire club fielded two debutants, including the goalkeeper, and so the Baggies strolled to an easy, but low key victory. Our goal scorers didn't even bother to celebrate.
The mood changed in the 87th minute. A small group on the halfway line spilt over onto the perimeter track and looked

around tentatively. Finding no opposition, they moved onto the pitch, immediately followed by hundreds more. The players ran for cover. Behind them were shameful scenes, as so-called Albion supporters deliberately swung en-masse on a crossbar until it snapped. The match was abandoned. It was a horrible end to a horrible season.

Up to that point, our protests had been lawful, and mainly dignified, but this badly crossed the line, thanks to a hooligan element. We'll never know what was said to whom and when but seemingly the incident was forgotten about once the Baggies piggy bank was raided to recompense Shrewsbury. The Baggies finished seventh. A 1-0 win at Peterborough during the run-in, rather than the goalless draw actually achieved, would have given them another shot at promotion. We were that close. Club history may have been quite different if Gould's squad had somehow won a couple more matches. With a promotion to his name, Gould would have kept his job and had the chance to re-shape the squad. After that, who could say? Promotion would have knocked the wind out of the Gould naysayers for a time but ultimately Gould and our venerable institution would have parted company. Better sooner rather than later. He might have taken his promotion bonus and then walked to take the Coventry job.

There was one final indignity. The Supporters Club Player of the Year event followed the night after Gay Meadow. It was then high profile when everyone at the club and supporters mixed freely. But the evening was ripped apart. Objecting to Malcolm Boyden's wit, Gould, plus his players and their partners rose almost as one and walked out. According to at least one source, some of the players ended up in the Hawthorns pub and involved in a drink-induced pub game which ended in several scuffles.

Before the blame game could get into gear the following day, John Silk rang Gould to sack him and then fell on his own sword. Looking back decades later, Gould reflected: *"Don Howe was right all along. I shouldn't have gone there in the first place."* Yep.

This season showcased fan power, in a manner which has never been fully repeated since. This power was a blunt tool, and sometimes used in a misguided way, but through dogged campaigning and persistence in the face of adversity, we'd collectively bought about change. Not just the managerial choice, but it also sent a strong message that more thought had to go into the position of Chairman.

Only days after the demise of Gould and Silk, Trevor Summers became the new Chairman, and Ossie Ardiles the new gaffer. The wave of optimism felt almost visible.

92 93 More of the Same?

Ossie Ardiles was a first-class fit for the Baggies. His image, his philosophy, his array of medals and pedigree matched Albion's history and ambition perfectly. Although Bruce Rioch and Ian Ross were also interviewed, there was only going to be one winner. He'd played for four English clubs, and managed two but inevitably every pen picture highlighted Ossie being a key member of the 1978 Argentinian World Cup winning team. He had a World Cup winners' medal, for heaven's sake, more than sufficient to give him an impenetrable aura. He was beyond criticism for supporters and players alike, despite a previous distinctly average record of winning matches. Ossie had the top trump and no-one in the UK could better him in the "put your medals on the table" challenge. That Ardiles should be willing to work in the Third tier of any national League was remarkable – albeit not unique. Former team mate Mario Kempes also managed several clubs with similar modest status. It said much for this educated, self-effacing, laid-back man who by example ridiculed the tabloid stereotypes of Argentinian people. He really just wanted to fit in. For instance, even though he knew nothing about the game, Ossie agreed to turn out in a cricket match for WBA. He was unconcerned that his leopard skin underpants glowed brightly through his 'whites' all evening. Our new man initially held his counsel on the state of the club. Two months had elapsed before he felt able to say *"Albion were a shambles when I arrived. They had just witnessed the most traumatic season in their history. The players were afraid to go out and play football. They knew that if they made a mistake, the crowd would have a go at them."*
His terms and conditions were verbally agreed with Chairman Trevor Summers. That pen, paper and ink were absent from the process was not a problem according to the Shedmeister.

Ardiles had shaken hands on the terms and "*being a gentleman*" a written contract was just a detail. But Ossie, like many professionals, had learnt the hard way about looking after Number 1 and the value of "Chairman's promises". Earlier that year, Newcastle Chairman John Hall said "*I have had long talks with Ossie Ardiles about what is needed – and let's kill off once and for all rumours that his job as manager is on the line. If he leaves the club, it will be of his own volition.*" Three days later, Ardiles was sacked.

With so many contracts running out, a large scale summer exodus from the Hawthorns naturally followed. Big earners Colin West and Graham Roberts plus local teenager Stewart Bowen (who joined his "mentor" Bobby Gould at Coventry) were among the 14 departees for whom written contracts were highly significant. Graham Harbey was actually sold for money. Albion's bank manager capered excitedly. Fortunately, with a new man in charge, Bernie McNally was persuaded not to retire.

The exodus created crucial wriggle room. The statement-making new arrivals included Ian Hamilton from 4th Division Scunthorpe United (£170,000) and full back Steve Lilwall from non-League Kidderminster in exchange for £60,000. Both were Burkinshaw 'spots'. Ossie was confident enough to say he'd "*never seen Lilwall play or heard of him.*" The Tatters kindly gave us keeper and Freddy Mercury lookalike Tony Lange for free. "*At Wolves, it was all long ball*" explained Lange, who clearly had lessons in how to make Albion friends. Closer to the big kick-off, there was a partner for SuperBob in the form of 32 year old battle-scarred veteran Simon Garner for thirty grand. When fit, Garner looked class but he was almost the last of his breed, an old fashioned footballer who smoked both before and after matches. Our apprentices openly goggled at his habits.

There was an infectious new buzz about the Hawthorns. Club

shirts were available in volume before the season started, which in itself created major excitement. The design, quickly nicknamed the 'bar code' because of the random width of its blue stripes, had many critics yet almost 2,000 shirts were sold in just four hours. It was all hands to the pump in those conditions, and to his credit Chairman Trevor Summers pitched in. Such "hands-on" was then (and still remains) a revelation. Albion Chairmen are normally aloof, remote people. His presence stoked up a David Cameronesque *"we're all in this together"* feeling. Summers decided he would become a full time Chairman to make quicker decisions ... or, more negatively, quicker interference. Because of his many years selling garden sheds, he was nicknamed "Fred the Shed." Fred's enthusiasm and stream of new ideas were both praiseworthy, but his financial track record in business was not exactly outstanding. Nor was he too hot on political correctness. His quip of *"spending your husband's money again"* as he took cash from Glynis Wright was comic – comically bad. At the time, Glynis earned twice as much as I did.

The football club remained in a bad place financially. Accounts showed commercial income dropping by 22%, a shocking figure when every penny counted. The Commercial manager resigned. His replacement, Tom Cardall was quite candid that he'd inherited a mess. Lurid rumours did the rounds over what the outgoing regime had or hadn't done to whom and in which bedroom. The truth was out there somewhere. The miserable figures, plus the worst season in the club's history, led to prominent shareholders declaring they wanted new blood on the Albion Board. With three directors requiring re-election, a power struggle was underway.

Albion had plans to make the Smethwick End all-seater, but no money. The knackered roof could wait no longer and so the famous old stand lost its cover for a full season. In private, the club admitted they couldn't afford to begin work until they were promoted and able to access grants available for second tier clubs. There were concerns that the ultimate ground capacity of 25,000 seats wouldn't be sufficient for a successful club. In response, a fanzine editorial asked *"why does our cynical nature suggest that if we were in the Premier League, the prices would be so high that there wouldn't be more than 25,000 who could afford it."* In any case, the Premier League seemed an awful long way away for a Third Division outfit.

To admire both new management and players, over 2,000 people descended on Evesham United's little ground, setting a new attendance record. Turnout for friendlies eased a little after that, but managing expectations was clearly going to be as challenging as the previous season. The new style of passing football drew much admiration, but needed to be allied to winning football. The reshaped squad were already mentally being assessed against the desperation for promotion.

The Tatters and the Bluenoses were in the Division above, with Villa in the new Premier League. We were the butt of so many pub jokes and our counter-arguments of cheaper admission, more victories and new grounds were ridiculed. It wasn't just our local rivals eager to twist the knife. I fell into conversation with a group of Tranmere Rovers supporters at a motorway service station. One of them quipped: *"do you realise that if West Brom play really, really well this season, then they might be good enough to play Tranmere next year."* Ouch.

There were three home friendlies including Premier League Blackburn Rovers. Rovers had Alan Shearer in their ranks, a youthful striker signed at huge cost from Southampton. In best Albion tradition, we tried to wind him up. *"What a waste of money"* we bravely chorused before being silenced by

Shearer's 25 yard strike. He added another in the second half. OK, we got the point!

The League opener was rather pleasantly at home. Blackpool were newly promoted from the basement division, and fancied their chances. Included in their ranks was a young Trevor Sinclair and in the squad Russell Hoult.

Albion went 2-0 up but the Seasiders fought back and halved the deficit. Shakespeare missed an Albion penalty. Blackpool then won a penalty themselves, but Bruiser Naylor admirably saved it. SuperBob wrapped up the win late in the game. It was a win, but far from a comfortable one, the first of many fiercely-fought fixtures.

Scapegoats were still sought in certain quarters. Young Roy Hunter, even though he was playing out of position, was deemed by some as *"the one to boo"* against Blackpool. In another sad sign of the times, the Brummie Road entrances was plastered with National Front stickers.

The first away match – at Huddersfield – was all-ticket until we arrived at Leeds Road, whereupon it became pay-on-the-day. This practice was irritating, confusing and unnecessary with an attendance of 8,000 in a famous old stadium capable of holding 20,000+. This was the Baggies first tough challenge and they came through it well, with Garner scoring the game's only goal. The whole team remained pleasingly unflustered throughout. Two games, two wins ... *"We are Top of the League"* was chorused from the open away end. Ossie's dream was very much intact.

Not for the first time, the Baggies made a quick exit from the League Cup. Being drawn against Plymouth over two legs was cruel on Baggies supporters. Around 700 travelled for the deciding leg at Home Park. Birthday boy Peter Betteridge was determined to be among them. On his 32nd birthday, Peter was one of a dozen supporters left behind at the Hawthorns as 4 coaches headed south to Plymouth. None had pre-booked, but the club imagined a minibus could be arranged for them. This didn't materialise, so while the majority gave up, Peter and three others remained determined. Hiring a car from a nearby depot was a possibility. Only Peter (a nervous driver) and one of the other three had a licence, and that was littered with points. So the birthday boy had to be the named driver and then there was another snag. The depot wanted £200 deposit. Peter had that sum but none of the others would or could help so Peter caught a bus into West Bromwich to get the cash. Upon his return, he found all his would-be accomplices gone. After much deliberation, he hired the car and was faced with a 200 mile drive in less than three hours, a tough call even for a confident driver. Peter got lucky. He even found a convenient parking spot and got inside Home Park after 25 minutes play though he was down to his last 25p. As he privately suspected, Albion were muscled out of the match and lost on aggregate. His return trip in heavy rain was even more unpleasant. Happy birthday, Peter! He didn't prang the car and got his deposit back next day. It was the least he deserved.

Back in the League, Bournemouth and then Stockport were

beaten at home. The slick demolition of County felt like revenge for the previous season's defeat. Garner scored two of Albion's three goals against the Cheshire men. Later, he reflected in the Albion News *"Being a striker, the way Ossie wanted to play, it was made for us because you knew there would be loads of chances coming up. I think the big thing was it got the supporters onside as well, they really enjoyed it."* Most of them did but one disgruntled visitor splashing through the Birmingham Road Gents at half time during the Stockport match was heard to moan *"I haven't been for twelve months because the Albion am crap. And they're still crap so I'm going home."* And he did, squeezing through the emergency turnstile to the sound of dropping jaws.

For everyone else, the bandwagon needed riding. At Fulham, Albion were a pleasure to behold, making second-in-the table Londoners look a rustic second-best. Fulham's opportunistic goal set up by 36 year old Steve Archibald, a previous scourge of the Baggies in his Tottenham days, prevented a victory. The draw was greeted with warm applause as it was deemed a good point against fellow promotion chasers. Yet twelve months earlier the same result prompted only protest. Supporters' mindset was black and white – Ardiles Good and Gould Bad, with no acceptance that both managers were really somewhere in between. As if to confirm the status of our diminutive Argentinean, he was voted Manager of the Month for August. Maybe the Football League hierarchy also wanted to meet him to enjoy some reflected glory.

After a grim struggle, Mark McGhee's Reading were the next visitors put to the sword at the Hawthorns. Top of the League Albion now had 16 points from the first 18. Nothing to this Third Division lark! In these pre-internet, pre-blanket TV days, it was an easy conclusion to reach. The regulars knew better. The team's form was patchy with their sporadic periods of brilliance being just enough to get them through and the squad was too small for comfort. Not all the faithful were content with the Ardiles-induced square passes across the back four waiting for space to emerge. *"Get it up there"* and *"don't prat around, get it forward"* were the more repeatable comments from the impatient brigade.

Given the results so far, following the team on a midweek trip to Burnden Park was essential. I was half-way through a residential training course at Chester but figured the Albion needed my presence. I was less cynical then.

Comparisons with the 3-0 defeat here twelve months ago were inevitable. Albion were again very much on the receiving end. But, full of confidence, Ardiles' Stars in Stripes defended well on occasions, and were just plain lucky on others. Against the run of play, SuperBob's Astle-like header gave us a lead. In shock, Wanderers folded, and Albion cruised home in style with Bob Taylor adding his 8th of the season close to time. The three points felt like six, with the bouncing away end doing our best to maximise noise. Few feelings in football are as uplifting as an away victory against the odds. Captain "Shakey" agreed. *"You'd have thought we'd won the FA Cup."* Ever the pragmatist, Gary Strodder added *"We've proved a point to ourselves, our fans and Bolton supporters."*

Stoke City was then, as now, the acid test. The Lardy Men looked a big barrier despite being 17th in the table. (Leyton Orient supporters decided that the large volume of portly City supporters was due to their eating lots of lard – hence the name).

Even though a decade without an away win at the Victoria Ground had passed, we believed this could be our day to beat the Lard-lovers. The Albion army was nearly 7,000 strong. We believed. Such was the volume of support, the Albion team coach couldn't fight their way to the Vic until 2.10pm. Unfortunately the infamous Mr Parker was in charge again, the same myopic individual that could see no evil with the

Torquay Kamikaze squad the previous season. The odds-on Championship favourites were matching Stoke, we really were, until Albion had one and then the other full back carried off, each a victim of lunging boots. Mr Parker again saw nothing wrong. He really should have gone to Specsavers. Despite a patched up defence and a slender lead, Ossie still naively urged his men forward. The outcome was a spectacular but seriously annoying 4-3 defeat. Here was a reality check for everyone that Ossie's team could be outmuscled, and would be vulnerable to swift counter attacks. Defeat was numbing.

WBA reported Parker to the Football League for swearing. Naturally, a few hacks made cheap copy from that, but as the Baggies discreetly pointed out; Parker booked Albion men for expletives yet swore himself at a player appealing to let the physio attend the mugged Lilwall. Parker was suspended, which acted as some meagre consolation for the defeat. Captain Shakespeare was as blunt as he dared in print *"Parker showed no discretion and was inconsistent."*

The perennial mickey-takers Exeter City were next in town. But with Ossie in charge, we could laugh off the bellowing Devonians, who'd waged recent literary exchanges through the Sports Argus letter pages. They were still the "*new kids on the block*", apparently, and Albion the '*fading old stagers*'. But on the day, the "new kids" offered nothing more than high work rate, blanket defence and bared teeth. Albion were on top and scored in the first half, though the quality of the final ball prevented more goals. Fanzine editor Glynis Wright had particular reason to jump about after Albion's first goal. She'd just been stung on the knee by a wasp, who'd determinedly buzzed up her trouser leg.

With Albion only clinching the game in the last minute, there was still room to argue that the Baggies hadn't fully recovered from their Stoke bruising. Still, on a more positive note, the editors of the Exe-Directory wrote in glowing terms about the warmth and generosity of Albion supporters they'd met.

Visiting Turf Moor was a League novelty not experienced since 1970, and was eagerly anticipated. Burnley were the reigning Fourth Division Champions, having just ended a seven year spell in the basement division. A few years earlier, they'd avoided relegation to the Conference on the last day of the season.

Few of our 2,500 strong following were aware of the hostility shown to visitors though Grorty Dick fanzine did its best to sound warning notes. Pre-match, the atmosphere was tense, with gangs outside every local pub eyeballing visitors as if they came from another planet. On the pitch, Burnley scored in the first minute. Their keeper, Marlon Beresford, was having one of those days when everything stuck in his hands. Once Conroy doubled their advantage, we all knew the game was up. Beating the League leaders at home ought to be cause for peaceful celebration yet perversely, Burnley supporters were in fighting mood.

The post-match violence was so intense that some supporters

to this day still refuse to travel to "the Turf". It was hard to grasp why our followers were widespread targets after the match. Anyone in an Albion shirt was fair game – in a car, walking up the road, or queuing in the chip shop. Even families and young children were harassed and punched in what was the worst display of violence in the town for at least four years. The Burnley hooligan mob broke their alleged 'code of conduct'. Their convoluted logic appeared to be that Burnley wanted revenge on Simon Garner who allegedly funded a small plane to fly over Turf Moor in 1991. Burnley were losing to Torquay in a Fourth Division play-off match when Turf Moor was buzzed at half-time by a plane trailing the message: 'Staying down 4 ever, luv Rovers, Ha Ha Ha.' A generation later and planes with mickey-taking messages still remain popular in the North West.

On the morning of the match, I travelled with the WBA Supporters team who played a team of Clarets in nearby Colne. The match was close, and played in a great spirit but more significantly, the pitch was just yards away from Colne Dynamos ground. The Dynamos were a very old but small club with a primitive ground. A local millionaire took them over and financed an all-professional team in an amateur League. Dynamos won every game easily, but to progress further required a new stadium. This was a tricky issue to resolve. The millionaire quickly tired of the waiting and closed the club instead. It was a then-shocking example of an historic institution becoming a rich man's discarded toy.

Ossie secured the September Manager of the Month award, his second on the trot. It simply felt wrong. On top of a mounting injury list, we'd lost two games in the last three, with worse to follow. Albion's passing football came unstuck again – this time against a resilient lower mid-table Port Vale. The other Potteries mob had a game plan to flood midfield and block off Albion's full backs. It worked and Vale pinched the points with a swift counter attack.

The gloomy mood continued at Springfield Park, Wigan. A fanzine poll later rated this museum piece as the worst in the Division. Surely the King Jeff Astle had Wigan in mind when he commented *"some of the grounds I've been to this season have made me cry."*

Ardiles' men were once again outmuscled and outrun. Erratic refereeing didn't help their cause. Standing behind a high fence on an open terrace in teeming rain was pretty close to making the 2,000 strong following feel as tearful as the King. That's without *"this bloody awful performance"* as the Grorty Dick match reporter described the 90 minutes. Such was Albion's increasing desperation that they resorted to the long ball, but without success as they lost their third straight away match. *"Crap ground, crap people, crap result"* lamented regular Graham Jones.

The moans and groans were rising in volume. *"It aye no better than Gould"*. We'd seen a glimpse of the Promised Land, but our TV was on the blink. With Bob Taylor's partner Simon

Garner more often injured than not, and Gary Robson off form, the team struggled to finish the numerous chances that were created. Robbo admitted *"for the past three or four matches, our trainer has been on the pitch more than the other side. We've picked up cuts and bruises all over the place – to the head, legs and body. Somehow we've got to start mixing it a bit more."*

There was no easy solution. Albion's financial problems hadn't gone away. Wages in 1991/92 exceeded total gate income. In addition, one pound in every five at the turnstiles was reserved for The Old Bill bill. Promotion, even if achieved, would be a double-edged coin. Income would rise but large promotion bonuses would need to be paid. Worse, once back in the second tier, the clock would start ticking on Albion's three-year expensive all-seater mandate. As new Director Terry Guy admitted *"Directors are working part-time. They mean well but things are getting overlooked and overlapped."* Albion had to accede to the bank's demand that no new players would be bought until others were sold.

Another name had just been added to the squad – Kevin Donovan for £70,000 from Huddersfield Town – while paying Winston White to make him go away didn't help much either. The bank had probably put their foot down after the Baggies had "boldly" bid £100,000 for a striker (Notts County's Kevin Wilson) – money they didn't have or had any possibility of obtaining any time soon. Fortunately for the balance sheet, County wanted double so the idea faded away. Also, Port Vale reported that we'd bid £250,000 for Peter Swan, ironically enough.

Albion's lot suddenly looked better at Hull City. Garner started but predictably had to leave the field prematurely, and City equalised with only three minutes left. Cue mass frustration on the narrow terrace steps.

Step forward Darren Bradley. Richard Brentnall takes up the

tale. *"Bradley's Airtours Special charted an unlikely path through the Humberside atmosphere and descended towards its touchdown. Keeper Fettis was horror personified as he first teetered backwards like Private Godfrey in the "Dad's Army" cricket match, arms spread-eagled, then looked for all the world as though he was seeing a plane coming overhead to crash nose-first into his upstairs bedroom. Did Darren really intend it, this forty-yarder from the right touchline? Who cares? It was a lovely moment to stand crushing, late disappointment on its head and snatch back the spoils from the jaws of denial, all the more lovely because it so rarely happens."*

The beautiful late win saw the Baggies elevated to top spot and Bradders made the subject of many questions. *"Of course I meant it. That's my story and I'm sticking to it"* he answered but always with a big grin.

To help move the Baggies out of their non-scoring rut, a loan deal was hastily assembled to bring in Luther Blissett to replace the stricken Garner. Blissett was in semi-retirement in Watford reserves, and agreed to turn out for the Baggies short-term as a big favour to Ossie Ardiles. He made his debut against Rotherham. The Millers as usual were high on grit and workrate. The Baggies fought back from a goal behind to take the lead, but United spoilt the celebration with a late equaliser. There was much muttering about *"too much fancy football in our own half."*

Fellow promotion contenders Hartlepool fancied a second straight win at the Hawthorns. They'd not lost away from home all season. In a titanic struggle which proved that 'Pools were not lower division mugs, both Gary Robson and Luther Blissett remembered how to finish. The Baggies remained top of a very tight pile with ten clubs split by only four points.

New boy Kevin Donovan was making a positive impression. He completed and refined Albion's midfield diamond. Donovan was at the front or "in the hole" linking up with the front men and running into gaps. Darren Bradley was at the back of the diamond in the forerunner of what is now called the defensive midfield shield. Between the pair were any two of Ian Hamilton, Craig Shakespeare, Gary Robson or Bernie McNally. The formation was much lauded, and it sounded revolutionary, even though Ossie had used exactly the same system at both Swindon and Newcastle. However the participants in Albion's diamond lacked pace, had limited tackling ability and were vulnerable to swift counter attacks. Ossie had a solution, even though it tried the bank's patience once more. He returned to his favourite Blackburn well to sign a free transfer tough tackling midfielder or defender called Reid. Two decades later, Robbie Di Matteo was to do the same thing. Ossie explained; "we've got to start winning the ball more often in midfield. You've got to win it before you can pass it and play." The expression "preaching to the converted" sprang to mind; not that supporters were complaining about new cheap muscle. The theory was sound yet due to injuries, Nicky Reid only played right wing back for the Baggies, a tough call for a mature player not blessed with pace. "I was up and down like a fiddlers elbow," he admitted many years later to the Albion News.

An FA Cup home match against Aylesbury was a blessed diversion from League matters. It was a pleasant diversion once the Baggies had got their nose in front. The unfortunate Non-Leaguers were run ragged, with Kevin Donovan scoring three of WBA's eight goals without reply.

The Baggies improved form was another false dawn. Albion's rose garden was still too easily trampled over. Fellow promotion hopeful Leyton Orient's muscular approach saw them defeat WBA 2-0. The match was memorable for a highly impressive away following of 3,000, and a quite shocking miss by Luther Blissett.

Now we understood Luther's nickname of "Miss-it" wasn't just a playful mickey-take. The mood was grim and a new scapegoat was created.

Although the genesis of "Boing Boing" is often disputed, the most vociferous school of thought has it this miserable afternoon in East London was the first time our unique ritual was observed. This observation seems hard to corroborate. I was at Brisbane Road and I don't recall any Boinging but one account suggests the Boinging was on a Sealandair coach rather than the terracing. Another school of thought claims 'Boing Boing' was first heard at Deepdale. The intrigue is fitting for an ancient club who, to this day, can't be certain where their nickname "The Baggies" stems from. Defeat to Orient felt like another Gould throwback.

Ah, yes. Mr Gould. One of the familiar Black Country pub debates was *"what would you say to Bobby Gould if he was here now?"* The response invariably depended on the volume of supped ale. Ian "Patch" Partridge from Warwick Branch WBASC actually had the opportunity at the frozen chicken counter at Sainsburys in Leamington Spa. Ian didn't hesitate for a moment. *"I want a word with you"* he demanded of the trolley-pushing Gould. *"What have you done to my team? You bought the wrong bloody Williams, didn't you? You haven't got a bloody clue..."* Normal supermarket business slowed down. Trolleys slid to a halt. Cashiers stood up to get a better view. Gould tried a variety of tactics to hold back the tide, and eventually Patch's red-faced girlfriend dragged him away. But Patch hadn't quite finished. He saw the former Albion man loading groceries into his red BMW, drove up behind him and hooted his horn. Gould's feet literally left the ground in shock - and Patch didn't stop smiling for three days. The passing of time has lent slightly sinister overtones to this anecdote but then Ian's exploits created only mirth.

While the Baggies were being bullied, the next visitors to the Hawthorns, Bradford City, had sneaked into top spot. Assisting City manager Paul Jewell was one Stuart Pearson. His insight into the Baggies squad, combined with monsoon conditions, helped City escape with a 1-1 draw. Bradford was to be Pancho's last managerial or coaching role, which implies that Gould may have been correct. His timing remains appalling.

The revamped Albion Board were in need of some decent PR after a public bloody re-election battle. There were only a few hundred shares in WBA, generally held within families. If any became available, the asking price was in excess of £2,000. Club rules ensured that no one person could own more than five shares. This anti dictatorship safeguard created instead a rotten borough. Showing the determination that would serve him well for decades, Joe Brandrick hung onto his seat but one of the more eloquent Board members, Mike McGinnity, lost his to local accountant Terry Guy. McGinnity's departure removed Trevor Summers' biggest critic.

As part of their master plan to move the club forward, the Board promised a PR Committee. It was launched with some pomp and numerous speeches before 200 curious supporters at West Bromwich's Gala Baths. In response to a question, Trevor Summers was adamant there was money to spend. Either he was extraordinarily badly-informed, or he was simply talking porky-pies. There was no money. The bank's ban on incoming players was quickly made public. The classic rules of PR are either "be honest or don't get found out". Fred the Shed failed on both counts.

All the Committee members, including Jeff Astle, Ray Barlow, myself and a few other supporters were co-opted in a classic box-ticking exercise. Despite prompting, there was no mention of elections, feedback mechanisms or any kind of formal structure. The Committee limped along, mainly behind closed doors, for a year or so before mercifully fading away. I seemed to be the only person asking repeated and pertinent questions or canvassing supporter opinion, neither of which were welcomed.

The Second Round FA Cup draw was unkind. Very unkind - an away draw to an outstanding Non-League club. Wycombe Wanderers were runaway leaders in the Conference and unbeaten at home for 14 months, where they averaged three goals per game. Their manager was a youthful Martin O'Neill. Like Ossie in the FA Cup, our knees had gone all trembly. Woking was on our minds.

Satellite channel BSkyB immediately scented blood, and had the match switched to a Sunday lunchtime kick-off. The TV fee was vital new revenue, provided we could grab it without the stench of defeat. Our 1,800 ticket allocation was quickly sold, though the club didn't do their fan base any favours by expecting supporters to queue on Monday morning at the Hawthorns, first come first served.

In the meantime, there was the horror of Preston's bum-numbing plastic pitch to negotiate. In theory, Albion's passing game should have been ideally suited for an artificial surface, particularly against struggling opponents. No-one was fooled. The best passing team in the Division struggled to control the bouncing ball on the hard surface. A late goal by Gary Robson saved a point.

The facilities at Deepdale had horrors of their own. With no top on the cistern, there was a free cubicle wash for every lady at no extra charge as Jean Zoeller discovered the wet way. Meanwhile in the Gents, the stainless steel urinal overflowed providing a free liquid shoeshine. Oh, the joys of the Great British Football toilet, where supporters wash their hands before going in.

The Buckinghamshire (almost) High Noon Sunday Showdown was next. Away supporters couldn't gain access to the small social club at Adams Park and the nearest pub was a mile away and as crowded as a Tokyo tube train. Thus a steady stream of Albion fans in need of a nerve-calmer resorted to an off-licence. Numerous small groups wandered towards the ground supping from assorted cans. Fortunately the Police were unconcerned. More and more mobile drinkers followed them, lager or beer in hand. And then one passed me drinking from a wine bottle. Wasn't that a tad upmarket? I couldn't help asking. *"They ran out of beer"* explained the fan. *"It's all gone. They're buying anything now. The bloke behind me got Head and Shoulders."*

The Baggies were attempting to live up to their name by sporting a new green and yellow strip with long shorts. It was rumoured their purpose was to cover Steve Lilwall's bandy legs. The not-so-short-shorts looked cumbersome, but didn't appear to inhibit their owners, who played with style and took a two goal lead into the interval.

The intense relief wasn't to last. First we lost Robson to food poisoning, and then Bradley to a knee injury. The latter injury necessitated bringing on Paul Williams. It was the strikers' final appearance before we finally found a fee small enough that Stockport were willing to pay to take him back. In goal, Bruiser Naylor was trying to make saves one-handed, later explained by a chipped bone in his other arm.

Albion's play became disjointed and Wycombe stormed at us in alarming fashion. They scored twice and Albion had to hang on nervously for a replay. No-one realised it at the time, but a second game was the best financial outcome, and later indirectly played a significant role in the end of season run-in. Bobby Gould was the "expert" talking head for the Sky commentary team perched in a high temporary platform. The Albion support was in terrific vocal form at Adams Park. We were only too willing to spare a thought for our ex-manager or even several thoughts. Gould's sexual preferences were queried, so too his eyesight, parentage and the size of his eyebrows. Oh, there was much verbal frustration and no little imagination let rip that afternoon. Sadly, nobody was able to get close enough to remove the ladder to the box. The sideshow was generally good humoured, with no more than a slight edge so being described as "*yobs*" by our own club Chairman was too much to take in without sitting down abruptly. Once again, Trevor had shown the gravitas of the local boozer loudmouth.

After the all-out Cup action at Wycombe, the League fixture at Swansea ended in a frustrating Friday night goalless draw. The Welsh flooded their midfield to such good effect that neither goalkeeper deserved their match appearance bonus. "Sicknote" Garner was injured again. His "free" transfer was starting to look expensive. The two points dropped left us seven behind the leaders, and still with the distraction of the Cup to deal with.

Earlier, the Albion supporters' coaches had endured their own frustrations. The Swansea Police tested out their low speed capabilities to meet Welsh MOT standards. The four miles under escort took an extraordinary 40 minutes yet at no point were any vehicles stationary. Fast walkers could have kept up. Probably the most memorable part of the trip were the so-called facilities. The toilets at the Vetch made you retch. Every trip, there were new indignities and the home end was no better. This time, we had a dimly lit brick structure with headroom barely six foot high. Thus, six-foot-two student Mike Jarvis emerged blinking into the daylight with brick dust in his hair, so much dust that some of it landed on the person next to him.

The interest in the FA Cup replay v Wycombe was remarkable, supporters or "yobs" being undeterred by normal prices for a midweek live game against Non-League opposition. Nearly 18,000 people were inside the Hawthorns. Albion's bank manager probably jigged with delight. The attendance included one Glynis Wright who should have been at work. She gambled on a colleague covering for her, that senior management would keep out of the way and that her face wouldn't end up on the TV. There was a narrow squeak when a Sky camera crew entered the Woodman pub. Who was that zooming towards the Ladies like Road Runner? Glynis!

Conversely, one Bobby Gould who had expected to be at the ground on commentary duties, was absent. Chairman Summers had used mouth without engaging brain and banned him. According to the Shedmeister, he could not guarantee that Gould wouldn't be physically attacked because of said "yobs" at Wycombe. And we called Gould eccentric? The King said "the ban was petty and unnecessary." Even club employee Ossie Ardiles called the ban "stupid and unnecessary." Gould milked the ban, forming an unlikely alliance with infamous journalist Steve Tudgay to trumpet the injustice. He claimed he even wrote to the Prime Minister. The West Midlands Police made an official apology but "six-gun Summers" blazed away again "disassociating WBA from the apology." When I challenged Summers about his unfortunate choice of words, he blamed the press for distorting his thoughts.

The public spat distracted from the match, which dangled a Third Rounder against second tier West Ham as the prize. It was vital revenue for the hard-up Baggies, They'd already amassed £100,000 from the two gates alone, plus the TV fee, but playing the Hammers would double their money. Wycombe, backed by 4,500, wouldn't give in easily and demonstrated just how well they could defend. It was annoying their key defender Andy Kerr hailed from West Bromwich, attended George Salters School and was an Albion supporter. The team he supported looked nervous, with Woking on their mind and the deadlocked match headed towards extra time.

Glynis simply had to get to work by ten o'clock and so had a dilemma looming, not least because her husband had unhelpfully declared he was staying put. To her enormous relief and that of most of the crowd, Bob Taylor scored his 15th of the season late in the game. The Baggies just held on in the face of a ferocious late rally for "*the finest win of the season*" as Ossie called it. Glynis managed to get to work literally seconds before senior management could spot her absence. Meanwhile, as Craig Shakespeare put it *"the lads were physically and mentally shattered in the dressing room after the match. They'd been on a hiding to nothing."* O'Neill's men deserved their ovation from both home and away supporters alike, which led to a "thank-you" letter to the Baggies from the visiting team. Not bad for yobs, really. Wycombe went on to win the double of the Conference Championship and the FA Trophy.

After such an effort, Albion didn't need more awkward opponents in the League. They were fortunate that Mansfield Town were in ultra-negative mode. Even their own supporters booed them for their timid approach. The Stags defended with eleven men at the Hawthorns but the Baggies eventually managed a routine win.

Poor little Chester were the Boxing Day turkeys. City propped up the table and had no hope until the fog came down. Some fans didn't even bother to leave their houses, convinced that the match would be off.

A few matches in Albion's history are better remembered for weather than the game itself, and this affair added a whole new chapter. There was once a defeat at Molineux when only the inhabitants of the North Stand could actually see the goals. A recent home reserve match had been abandoned because of bad weather, but no-one remembered to tell the shivering supporters. Chester was in the same bracket. City protested that visibility were impossible. The referee believed he could see both linesmen from the middle of the pitch, and that was good enough for him.

Depending on their position in the ground, supporters could see either the Brummie Road or the Smerrick End goal, but not both. Still, we're only yobs not worthy of any opinion, so the match kicked off. Up in the gantry, Martin Lewis, commentating on the official club video, had an obvious problem. His solution was simple *"I just made it up figuring no-one would know any better..."* So on the full version of the video, the first half was described in lavish terms *"Albion's football is quite beautiful, it's the best I've seen this season. Oh just look at that for a pass... wonderful stuff...."* Check it out on YouTube. Back at ground level, less than half the attendance saw Paul Raven's first half goal, but as the teams lined up for the kick-off, Raves helpfully pointed to himself to indicate he was the goalscorer. *"Brummie, Brummie, what's the score?"* chorused the Smethwick Enders.

"1-0 to the Albion, 1-0 to the Albion" was the instant response. Of course, from that point on, the score became increasingly

fanciful from the imaginative Brummie Roaders who apparently saw 15 additional goals on top of the official 2-0 score.

Much was made in the media of the Baggies clocking up four straight clean sheets. The away Christmas match at Plymouth boosted the total to five – albeit with a goalless draw. There was little else to mention from the Home Park fixture on a pitch that resembled quicksand in places. The Baggies goals against column noted just 19 and only Manchester United in the whole country could better that. Ossie put the improvement down to defending set-pieces with greater numbers. What he found less easy to explain was why his Albion team had amassed four points fewer than Gould did from the same number of matches. Most sides couldn't cope with Ossie's fluent diamond at the Hawthorns, but away from home, team fluency was rarely in evidence. Since Albion had been knocked off the top spot in October, there had been no songs sung about promotion. The faithful were worried.

The Albion News advertised a plane trip to Plymouth, a novel idea. The organisers were an obscure company called Sportex, who made lots of promises in their advertising, but were unable to keep them. Some of the travellers complained of shoddy arrangements and worse a letter from the Sportex MD accused 40% of the travelling group of being ejected for foul behaviour. Grorty Dick fanzine took up the supporters' cause as Albion's "PR Department" predictably sided with their advertiser. Sportex hit back with a solicitors letter threatening court action for libel. After the fanzine assembled 26 witness statements from among the 50 who travelled, nothing was ever heard of Sportex again. The travellers had to take the experience on the chin but at least the publicity prevented a repeat performance both from Sportex and the Baggies. It wasn't the only time the club would jump into bed for a short-term buck, regardless of consequences.

The inspiration behind Sportex was to strike again later. He operated a similarly shabby scheme for taking Scotland supporters to a Euro '96 game at Villa Park. Later still, he featured on a BBC 'Watchdog' programme.

The FA Cup was still magic. The arrival of West Ham drew almost 26,000 and most thought the Londoners were beatable. But not for the first time, the Baggie boys were fazed by a big crowd. Long before the home side could exert any serious pressure, they were two goals down and out of the Cup. *"Outclassed"* wasn't too strong a description.

After Ossie confessed: *"we let supporters down badly",* the overall mood was downbeat. Did Ardiles' men really have sufficient stomach for the scraps ahead?   West Bromwich Albion had not won at home in front of a 20,000 crowd for 7 years. Ossie again: *"Some players are lacking confidence and need the support of the fans. It's vital that fans stay patient."* The comments and the mood both had echoes of the unrealistic but overwhelming tide of optimism back in the summer. The reality could not match the dream.

In early January, Billy "Popeye" Martin was knocked off his bike and killed by a coach near to Rolfe Street station. Billy was unique. There can never be another Billy, given the mutual suspicion nowadays between supporter and player. Despite being nearly 80, Bill attended all club training sessions and acted as ball boy, tea maker, emergency goalkeeper or any other function or odd job that the manager would permit. His fitness level and enthusiasm were both extraordinary. Keeping up with the players gave him no difficulty, always a source of mickey-taking among the squad, particularly for new signings. *"Reckon you're quick? How come that 80 year old has just run past you?"*

I went to Popeye's funeral, along with many other supporters and the entire squad. Unfortunately the service was just a standard affair, with insufficient weight given to an extraordinary, modest man. We all got more from the minute's silence at a home match, a rare but utterly deserved privilege for a supporter.

Bill was a Baggie all his life, watching games during Albion's 1919-20 Championship season and even outlined to me how he met Jesse Pennington in his shop during the great man's playing days. Craig Shakespeare summed up the feelings of the players: *"we all thought the world of Bill who will be remembered for his sense of humour and lovely nature."*

A 4-0 thrashing of Walsall in the Autoglass Trophy, days later, didn't convince anyone that our fortunes were changing. We all knew Albion could deal with the smaller clubs. One of the goals came from a Bob Taylor penalty. It was his first ever from the spot, and designed to get him scoring after a difficult time.

Bob's boost was timely. Bolton were in town. After a miserable start to the season, the Wanderers were unbeaten in 15 matches and a definite threat. They were sixth to the Albion's second spot but the difference in points was only four. The Baggies were in imperious form, shrugging off an early Bolton penalty and roared back to win in some style. Bob Taylor scored the final goal in a comfortable 3-1 win, his first League goal for almost three months. The dream was alive and kicking again.

The lure of the Autoglass Trophy took 400 gallant souls to Mansfield in midweek for a novelty fixture at a new ground. A vast open terrace did nothing to keep out the bitter cold. Having thrashed Walsall in the round robin stage, the Baggies were virtually already through to the next stage and fielded a very young team. The Stags, despite their dismal League position, had recently sold their best forward, leaving them with a top goal scorer with just three to his name. Their lack of prowess showed as Mansfield spent their evening lashing footballs in every direction bar the goal. Supporters were in more danger than the goal net. Each miss was greeted with more jeers and a noticeable scowl from Mansfield keeper Pearcey. An expert showed them the way – a SuperBob header was the only goal of the night.

The previous season, the computer gave us two Devon winter trips in a week. This time, the IT was kinder – with a two-week gap between the visits rather than one. We were off to the perennial mickey-takers Exeter City. We knew we'd be reminded that *"you're not famous anymore"* in what their fanzine gleefully referred to as a *"sustained period of mockery."* The fixture appeared to be another routine long-distance hike as St James was no longer a novelty. We all knew what to expect from City's ancient wooden non-smoking main stand. Following those loveable lardies from Stoke hurling hot drinks at Alan Ball, supporters were no longer permitted onto the running track at half-time to light up. A request for our supporters to be allocated the largest terrace, the comically-named "Big Bank", was predictably turned down, albeit on the spurious grounds *"that Albion are not a family club like Watford or Charlton".*

Thus we had the scruffy little terrace at the other end, woefully inadequate for the numbers who wanted to travel. The Gents toilets faced onto the street and had no glass in its windows. It was possible to have a conversation with passers-by and take care of nature's needs at the same time.

But this trip was different. The Grorty Dick crew met their Exe Directory counterparts for pre-match drinks in the excellent Victoria pub. Barriers eased down. Albion supporters weren't arrogant and, in return, there was much to be said for the community spirit of smaller clubs. The two fanzines sold side-by-side outside the away end and there was many a ticketless Albion supporter grateful for a timely intervention. The local Police were peddling the line that the match was all-ticket and sold out. Alan Crockford of the Exe Directory genuinely risked arrest for repeatedly pointing out that neither statement was true.

On the field, things were different too. Although we'd passed the ball around with much composure on the boggy surface, the decisive moves belonged to City. Twice Hodge had slung in quality crosses and twice Moran scored, one of them off Paul Raven. Albion's much vaunted defence was having an off-day. Exeter's fans were in their element. *"You might as well go home..."* we were taunted repeatedly. With only 20 minutes remaining, a few did just that. After all, the three points had gone. Nearly twenty years had elapsed since Albion last recovered from two goals behind to win.

And then ... Darren Bradley found Carl Heggs from fully 40 yards. Heggsy reacted quickly with a perfectly weighted shot over City keeper Miller into the top corner. Exeter wobbled, and then sagged three minutes later as Gary Hackett equalised from virtually the same spot as Heggs. In the space of 180 seconds, the game had turned round, and now it was the locals on the receiving end ... *"Go home, you might as well go home"* we bellowed with rare enthusiasm. The Grecians were under the cosh, unable to handle Bradley and Robson. They were simply panicking and no-one more so than goalkeeper Kevin Miller trying to stop SuperBob by kicking him in the ribs. Penalty.. plus a red card for Miller for the crude challenge.

Ian Hamilton later described the key moments to the Albion News. *"Bob had stayed down for ages and then limped around. In his bruised state, he didn't want to take the penalty. So I ended up doing it and I can see it now, putting the ball on the spot and it just sinking into the mud, thinking "Oh God, what have I let myself in for? But I scored and that gave me so much satisfaction because it was a great win."*

Great win? More than that, it was one of the best Albion games I've ever witnessed, before or since. The stunning novelty of the comeback, the new belief in the Ardiles dream and real evidence that the team included "diggers" as Hammy put it. Matches like that are rare and deserve to be treasured. Another treasured memory was the first ever public airing of the unique Taylor-Heggs celebration. Both players stood on one leg, threw their arms wide and then high-fived each other. It was a ritual best observed live and was the first of many. The Boinging continued long after the final whistle.

Supporting legend Dave "the Mammoth" Holloway recalled *"Exeter was the most amazing away match I have ever been to. Twenty minutes from the end, I wanted the referee to blow as I had had enough and then bang, bang, bang."*

For those who'd made their own way, it was back to the Victoria Inn once again. One communal *"Boing Boing"* was interrupted by a loud crack as a bench broke under the weight of a huge Albion supporter. Fortunately, the pub staff were unfazed. Three hours later, the celebrations were still continuing. Both sets of supporters were getting on so well that previous arch-tormentor Alan Crockford ended up wearing a Baggies shirt. Five minutes later, he threw up but chose to blame the shirt rather than the ten pints of strong cider he'd supped.

In a letter to Grorty Dick, mine host Donna from the Victoria expressed the thought that *"your lot were certainly fun to have around and certainly enhanced the reputation of the travelling football follower."* Not a word of recrimination about damage to an historic bench. Pensioner Norman Catton explained *"my Grandad hid under that bench during the Boer war, concealing himself from a press-gang "recruiting" for the army. He sat there through much of the First World War and again during the Second World War; though Exeter was very badly bombed, the pub remained unscathed, likewise the bench. That old seat survived everything until WBA came to town."* Oh whoops.

With Simon Garner crocked again – this time for a month – a little of the Cup windfall was invested in wages for another loanee. After failing to persuade one -club man Bernie Slaven to leave Middlesbrough, Albion secured yet another 32 year old who'd previously played for Blackburn – David Speedie. The arrival of Stoke City at the Hawthorns, backed by 9,000 trying to squeeze themselves through the turnstiles, contributed mightily to a near 30,000 gate. The meeting of First (unbeaten in 20) against Second (unbeaten in 8) captured the imagination and broadened the grin for the bank manager. There was a 7 point gap between First and Second place teams so, depending on the outcome, the gap could become manageable or unreachable.

It was the latter. Big game, big gate and the Baggies were second best again, just as the cynics predicted they would be. Once again, Stoke's physical strength and their big boots were too much. SuperBob was pushed, tugged and jostled. He looked in vain for support from the anonymous Speedie. As was so often during this period, irritating City striker Mark Stein was the difference. He scored the winner, probably with his hand, but that was typical of City's luck that term. Cue another mass chorus of bloody "*Delilah*", a miserable dirge which genuinely kept me awake.

Everyone knew then that Stoke were on the way to winning silverware, and the rest of us were only chasing one automatic spot, plus four places in the 'consolation cup'. Over 20 years had elapsed since the Baggies had played at the twin towers or a whole generation. For a so-called cup team, this was a miserable showing. "*Wembley, Wembley ... it's a place in London that we never get to see...*" was the ironic cry but (not even) deep down there was hurt each time another modest club secured their big day out. But much as an appearance at the twin towers was yearned, the desire for automatic promotion burned more strongly. The Play-offs were just too much of a gamble.

After the Stoke set-back, Albion had three less taxing matches in which to pick themselves up. The first was a miserable night, in almost every respect, at Bournemouth. Miserable weather, turnout and football, but there was the consolation of a ground out 1-0 win, courtesy of David Speedie. It was comparable in many ways to a Megson-type victory. Such matches can be quickly passed over if the next is an improvement. It wasn't.

Bottom of the table Huddersfield secured a 2-2 draw at the Hawthorns, probably much to their own surprise. Albion were two goals up after an hour. After two home matches without a win, the natives were in moaning mood. The team was booed off the pitch amid choruses of "*What a load of rubbish.*" The manager believed "*some of the players were uneasy playing at home*" which was a reference to a possible hangover from last season. Critics pointed out that wages and bonuses were higher than many clubs in the Division above, and if players couldn't cope with pressure, they shouldn't be in the game. Once again, the letters pages of the Argus were filled with variants on the familiar *"where's the money gone?"* Nobody suggested that Ardiles wasn't any better than Gould, even though League position was similar. Ossie's aura remained unshakeable.

West Bromwich Albion rarely have early or late season seaside trips. These are normally scheduled for the winter months and in midweek, just to maximise the irritation. So Blackpool on a Saturday in February seemed almost a mistake, and the Black Country hordes were determined to take advantage. The game was all-ticket. Bottom four Blackpool were grateful for any revenue, so happily gave the Baggies a 50/50 split of their 10,000 ground capacity.

Steve Sant was one of a 23-strong group from a Black Country pub who found a Saturday afternoon match at Blackpool the perfect excuse for a windy weekend. They commandeered a guest house and drunk it dry by 9pm on Friday night, so ventured out in the arctic gales. They were astounded by the sight of every pub in the town being swamped by Albion people. *"The Navigation pub had 'The Liquidator' on its juke-box which must have made the pub owners a four figure sum before they took a penny piece over the packed bar. "We sang our hearts out, drank until midnight and staggered en masse back to our digs singing, among others, 'The Lords My Shepherd'. Back at the guest house, our hosts had parachuted in several cases of Holsten Pils and so we drank yet more until dawn. Some of our group spent all of Saturday in bed. Unsurprisingly all of us who were there recall little of the game bar the size of our support and the result."*

Selling fanzines outside the tatty old ground, Glynis Wright was pounced upon by desperate supporters using the age old logic of 'woman-handbag – aspirins'. Glynis emptied an entire bottle of pills to alleviate the mass suffering.

It would be too predictable to suggest that the Albion side were rather under the weather themselves. Bob Taylor levelled an early Blackpool goal, but the whole team were guilty of over-elaborating. They hit woodwork rather than netting and went down painfully 2-1. The hung-over masses, who were mainly stationed on open terracing on another wet and windy day, were too miserable to be overly concerned. But as Richard Brentnall opined *"days such as this one illustrate graphically just why so many Albion fans dread the prospect of the play-offs."*

Pressed for comment, Ossie was feeling the heat. *"There's an air of fear over the club because of what happened last season. We seemed to lose confidence in ourselves and begin to defend too deeply."* But Albion's problem was that they couldn't defend either. He added *"There is money to spend on new players."* With the mood now darkened, speculative fanzine column inches were given over to other 32 year olds who'd played for Blackburn and were available. Meanwhile, there was a new arrival on the alternative reading scene with the appearance of "The Baggies". With classic bandwagon- jumping, it was initially described as an official club newspaper, although it was nothing of the kind. There was no club investment – either financial or otherwise, and the disillusioned editor Glenn Willmore was quick to declare UDI.

The newspaper was to become an intrinsic part of home matches for the next decade and a half. Indeed, with a newspaper sales team initially recruited via Smethwick Jobcentre, pavement space was becoming crowded alongside traditional fanzines Grorty Dick, Last Train to Rolfe Street and the short-lived Albion Chronicle. This was the golden age of unofficial publications. Combining forces to produce a "super fanzine" was an idea regularly raised by outsiders, however the differences in personalities and outlook were always too great to breach. Factionism has always been the lot of Baggie people. Witness the subsequent plethora of supporters clubs and the variety of travel organisations.

There is a football scenario when the "*brave little club*" become the "*ugly undesirables*" because of their tactics and attitude. Basement division Torquay United in the Autoglass fulfilled one role and then the other. The prize, if it could be called that, was an away match at Stoke City. Partly as a result, barely 5,000 turned up either out of a sense of duty or completism. There was much muttering in the ranks as Torquay scored early who then looked comfortable with their advantage. At first, the criticism was levelled at the Baggies' mournful showing but as the Devon side resorted to a Stoke-level of cynicism, the mood changed. United were endlessly time-wasting and feigning injury, or when all else failed tried to cut their opponents in half. The gallant 5,000 rallied in indignation, fired by their sense of injustice.

The game finally turned on an injury to the Torquay keeper, one Kevin Blackwell, much later of Sheffield United fame. He'd gone down in a heap again, but the referee, weary of his play acting, waved play on. The injury was serious and off went Blackwell. Amid much mickey-taking, "Albion reject" Adrian Foster went in goal for the visitors to replace the hamstrung keeper. Torquay were effectively doomed from that moment. With four minutes left, Kevin Donovan equalised with a header. It was celebrated wildly on and off the pitch as was the winner, also from Donovan, during injury time. Justice! Foster is mostly remembered for his part in the Twerton debacle. *"Foster, Foster, what's the score?"* roared a delighted Brummie Road End.

Prior to the League match with Fulham, Mickey Mellon was added to the squad. He cost £50,000 from Bristol City. Mickey was only 20, had never played for Blackburn, and had a reputation for being "hard." He made his debut against the Londoners, and scored the crucial third in an ultimately heartening 4-0 triumph. The victory was not straightforward. Fulham became quite rampant when two goals in arrears and the home side were hanging on.

Ossie tried to make a virtue of a necessity by playing a back five at Stoke for the Autoglass Quarter Final. And it worked. Well, nearly. The massed defence managed to contain Stein, and matched the Lardies muscle, albeit Fereday had to be carried off after a brutal challenge that predictably didn't even earn a yellow card. Stoke just had a problem with Albion full-backs.

The braced 3,000 Albion support, anticipating an onslaught, gradually dared to hope that the route to Wembley might still be open. Hope became joy when Bob Taylor gave us the lead. SuperBob went on to miss a one-on-one to secure the win - and the match went downhill from there. David Speedie, who had the potential to be Ardiles' Williams had his signing been permanent, was making a complete arse of himself. He was already being barracked for being a former Stoke player and multiplied this several-fold when he reacted to a foul against him by petulantly kicking the ball into the crowd. It struck a young boy. After that, I felt like booing him. Ten minutes from time, Cranson, resembling an excavator, clattered into Speedie for a sure fire penalty. But no spot kick was given – probably because it was Speedie. City immediately counter-attacked and Stein scored. Albion lost their composure, and Stein grabbed the winner during injury time. The experience was scream-inducing. The peons of praise for Mark Stein were still audible when I reached my car. Student Andy Price: *"I can't describe my feelings. I'm still numb inside. There's no excuse to collapse in the last ten minutes against any side, let alone in a Cup tie against a team who have already taken the piss by getting all 6 League points."*

The Baggies back five line-up was retained for the trip to Stockport. Once again, Bob Taylor gave us the lead and once again, the defence couldn't hold out. No, to be truthful, they fell apart. County's height and long ball game led to an embarrassing 5-1 defeat. Predictably, Paul Williams scored the final goal – a tap in – and celebrated wildly. The earlier interaction between player and the 2,500 Albion supporters didn't help anybody. Williams reacted to carrots hurled in his direction and abuse that he was Gould's nark by spitting at the away end and blowing kisses to the Stockport supporters. This was another depressing afternoon at Edgeley Park – arguably even worse than the 3-0 defeat under Gould 14 months earlier – and the parallels were overwhelming. Ossie's men were now fourth.

The general bad mood was reflected by the Stockport Police. They'd piled into the away end to arrest a supporter who had made pig noises at them. Yes, it was stupid and unnecessary, but an arrest? Such was the consequent level of abuse and fury directed at the Police, mass ejections were threatened. Several fellow supporters were so angry, they drove to the Police Station in central Stockport to make a complaint.

According to their account, they tried and failed for three hours to find any officer willing to pay attention to their concerns. After the match, a line of Police horses blocked off all seated Albion supporters from their coaches. The mounted Police ignored all requests, polite or otherwise to let us get past, so we had to find their own way. One supporter was kicked and at least two others were nearly crushed by horses backing into them and a wall. The Supporters Club later made a complaint but hey, we're only football supporters, and therefore second class citizens.

Keith Burkinshaw got his retaliation in first. *"As soon as we hit a bit of a bad patch, people started walking around talking about February this and February that. It's almost as if they are willing things to go wrong and there's no need for it."* An Albion side who couldn't score enough goals and conceded far too many was a recipe for sliding backwards down the table – just like last season. The side badly needed a partner for Bob and someone to get hold of the defence. But in the dressing room, Ossie remained calm and composed, if a little incoherent. Ian Hamilton *"Ossie was great when we did lose, he wouldn't rant and rave, he'd come in, nice and calm, just tell us to carry on playing as we were and that results would come."* Oh, that all supporters could be convinced that easily, particularly as the following Saturday a date awaited us at second in the table Port Vale

It is a football truism that Vale Park has its own weather system. Regardless of conditions at your home base, the climate in good old "Boslum" will be different. And it is rarely pleasant. I recall leaving the Black Country one evening in bright sun for a reserve game at Port Vale only to discover a blizzard in one of the Potteries five towns. The game was called off.

On this day, swirling wind combined with driving snow contrasted with the bright sunshine in the Black Country. A pain for photographers, but it was downright horrible for supporters and players alike, even though for the first time, the away end had a roof.

Albion did their usual trick of scoring first and losing. That the final score was "only" a 2-1 defeat came as no consolation. The writing was written in the blizzard long before Vale notched their winner. Ex Albion man Nicky Cross scored the first, and set up the second. Even Ossie admitted *"We stopped playing and stopped going forward. That was very unfortunate."*

Unfortunate. Our manager was instinctively demonstrating his legal background. The 5,000 Albion fans choose to use slightly stronger language after the Baggies fourth consecutive away defeat. *"No bottle!", "no stomach for a fight"* and *"can't handle big games"* were the more polite comments from supporters trying to make a speedy exit from the Potteries' answer to Bilston. The Albion team were barracked off the pitch. The Ossie aura was finally cracking. Local radio handled their first *"he's gotta goo"* calls.

Thankfully, Simon Garner was fit again. His return to fitness coincided almost suspiciously with the Burnley match. *"Simon Simon Garner"* only needed two minutes' action at the Hawthorns to score what was his 200th League goal. My, did he enjoy that. For once, the Baggies kept their opponents in check and won 2-0. Garner back, and a victory to celebrate? The world felt a better place.

Remember the lament about midweek seaside trips? The computer did it again, sending us on a Wednesday night to the Sussex home of Imitation Albion, name usurpers never to be taken seriously. The Goldstone Ground was a big ol' barn of a ground, with half of it being open terracing. It needed to be full to create any atmosphere, so a mere 7,000 attendees made for a subdued evening. The one thousand real Albion diehards had an enormous terrace all to themselves, surrounded by cold evening air and concrete. Albion were nervous, making mistake after mistake, but surprisingly this was play-offs hopeful Brighton making all the errors, not the visitors. As one wit put it *"they don't just look like Andy Pandy, they're playing like him as well."* Brighton wore blue and white striped shirts and shorts.

Eventually WBA took advantage through a Bob Taylor penalty. It should have been all the Baggies needed. But poor marking gave Brighton an equaliser and after that ... we all know what happens next, children. By the end, with Brighton celebrating their 3-1 victory, tempers snapped on the away end. Red-faced and furious, some fans were unable to deal with five largely unnecessary straight away defeats. Angry words were exchanged, retorts snapped back, and punches followed. Even then, there was some black humour – *"even the supporters have more fight about them than the team."* This was Ardiles' Hartlepool, an ugly rock-bottom where West Bromwich fans were reduced to fighting each other. Our dream of automatic promotion, and maybe even the consolation play-offs were surely dead. We were down to fifth, and apparently only able to collect points at home. The trip home was particularly long, tedious and quiet. There were no bouncy sound-bites from management. Just Burkinshaw's terse *"the truth is that we have got certain players that cannot raise their game when the heat is on."* Or, expressed in more basic terms," *no bottle."*

92-93 run-in - Proud to be a Baggie

It was wobbly West Brom's good fortune that back at our ranch, big and ugly Leyton Orient sought only a draw. The Londoners defended very well in what became a tedious, nervous affair. Eventually, a combination of Orient flagging and substitute Strodder replacing Garner up front created sufficient space for Burgess, and then Donovan, to secure another home win. We did home wins well. Albion rose to third, just two points shy of the automatic spot held by Port Vale. If only all our matches were at home!

 'Bruiser' Naylor became the fall guy for the most recent away defeat, losing his green goalkeeping shirt to Freddie Mercury. sorry. Tony Lange. The general downbeat mood was further accelerated by complaints about the Hawthorns admission prices in the local press. Others stridently pointed out that Ossie had just £100,000 to invest in new talent while the Blues, allegedly, had seven times that amount. All subscribed to the *"Albion has lots of money stashed away under their mattress that they ought to be spending"* theory.

The Baggies assistant manager was in forthright mood again. *"I've never known another club like this one. Everyone inside and outside the place seems to be waiting for us to fail, and it gets right up my nose."* Burkinshaw's blunt comments failed to acknowledge just how far the once-mighty WBA had fallen, with attendant regular doses of empty promises. The possibility remained that the club could finish in its' lowest-ever League position. Older supporters, who had savoured the glory days, could only see humiliation and embarrassment in the Third Division. Burkinshaw did admit: *"we have players who struggle to make the right decision at the right time."* Ossie was more pragmatic. *"The way we play away from home these days, teams don't beat us, we beat ourselves. I regard WBA as a patient that is ill. I am the Doctor who must decide what to do. If we are promoted, there'll be a routine operation. If not, the patient will require major surgery."* There was iron in those words and a warning for his players whose livelihoods were at stake. It's the managers' ultimate revenge. Next up... oh dear... another away game. The archetypal Third Division match too – a trip to the three sided Victoria Ground, Hartlepool. Rather like Port Vale, this ground has its own weather system but with the dubious benefit of the bitter North Sea. Craig Shakespeare was an experienced lower Division ground visitor. *"Even on a red hot day it would be blowing a gale. And the pitch would be awful."*

There was Third Division organisation, too. Hartlepool decided the game would be all-ticket, but then changed their minds before any tickets went on sale. Just four days before the game, they panicked and reverted to a ticket-only status. Cursing supporters had to make a special journey to the Hawthorns or reluctantly decide they couldn't go. On the Friday, it was back to cash turnstiles after all. Inspired.

The home side hadn't scored at home all year, which for bookies meant short odds on an away win. But we was Albion, and although there was rejoicing that the appalling Speedie had departed, there were many others feeling the downside of big support, big pressure.

For supporters unable to attend the previous midweek fixture, this was their first chance to visit the "Vic". The 2,000 away supporters made up half the gate, despite the Pools ticket confusion. Seated in the away end was Richard Ryan and his dislocated shoulder. He'd somehow found a way to drive himself one-handed nearly 200 miles, deciding that three different buses just to get to the coaches at WBA for a 9.00am start was even more hassle.

The seated Baggies with their low roof were better off than those standing on the open terracing. In late March, one might have hoped for mild-ish conditions but Hartlepool weather prevailed. *"The conditions were terrible, the pitch, the wind – everything"* lamented our man from South America, not that the shivering gallant travellers needed reminding.

Feeling the heat despite the chill, Albion's defence were creaking under only moderate long ball pressure. There were too many errors, including giving Pools a penalty. Andy Saville duly scored and there were predictably spectacular celebrations - hard to blame them after 1,200+ goalless minutes. The Baggies quickly levelled with a stylish move that Hamilton finished off, and then dominated without scoring. Cue for Hartlepool to score again through the suddenly prolific Saville and a sixth straight away defeat beckoned.

Ardiles' team were forced into an unlikely forward line of Taylor, Strodder and Ampadu. They conjured a series of near misses. With two minutes remaining, the ball ran out of play for what was probably a goal kick. But to a person, the seated Baggies supporters howled for a corner - and got it. The referee influencing proved crucial. Hamilton swung in the corner and Raven neatly headed a late equaliser. Oh, the relief! Richard Ryan leapt up with all the others punching the air with his damaged right arm... He confessed: *I've never celebrated an Albion goal by sitting down with a pained expression on my face but this was all I was capable of for a good few minutes."*

A draw was an improvement, but overall just showed up the

team's limitations especially as nearly all the other top sides had won. Albion relied on outscoring the opposition, but with Garner either unfit or just old and not-so Speedie hurled into the void, SuperBobby Taylor needed help.

Preston were midweek visitors to the Hawthorns. With all the top boys winning again the previous night, Albion were running to keep up. The metronome consistency of Stoke, Bolton and Port Vale was grinding everybody down. Still, it was a home game so confidence was high. John Beck's relegation-threatened team were quickly outplayed. Having to play on real grass, they were second best with the exception of their wide man, Lee Ashcroft. With his pace and trickery, the Baggies' two early goals didn't feel quite enough. Lilwall was booked for trying to block him and after that couldn't afford to take risks. Ashcroft exploited the extra yard and led a PNE recovery back to level the score. The moans and groans could be heard all around the stadium. *"Worst than bloody Gould... Swansea all over again.. will this club ever learn..."* and so on.

But just as at Hartlepool, there was a twist. Bob Taylor came to the rescue with a winner right at the end. It was a wonderful moment yet didn't quite seem real. The late goal was predictably seized upon as a symbol of hope by the optimists. The cynics were still lamenting how a two goal lead had been allowed to slip.

With just days to the transfer deadline and ten matches remaining, Ardiles rolled his last dice and signed a forward on loan from Newcastle – Andy Hunt. A modest fee of £100,000 was agreed, but the Baggies didn't have it, hence the temporary arrangement. The bank could be reassured that the outgoing would shortly be covered by the FA Cup TV fees. Albion were gaining a forward who was *"very mobile and exceptionally skilful with a strong left foot"* according to the gaffer. He also came cheap – Ardiles was straight with the player, explaining that such was Albion's relationship with the bank, they could offer only the same terms as Newcastle.

At 22, Andy sounded almost too young for an Albion team hitherto reliant on cheap senior temporary players. Ossie had made several approaches to his former club to sign the young striker. Keegan had previously always refused, but abruptly, the Geordies had the chance to make a signing of their own. As Hunt dryly observed: *"With Newcastle signing Andy Cole, you tend to get the idea you're on your way out."* Also one Andy Saville left Hartlepool to join Birmingham City. For 'Pools, the choice was to sell their star man or go into administration.

There was no time to introduce the newcomer gradually. Hunt was on the bench for the weekend fixture, away at Bradford City, which was switched to Sunday for live transmission on Yorkshire TV. Curiously, it was not available in the West Midlands. Partly as a consequence, 2,500 members of Ossie's army marched on West Yorkshire.

As regular travellers know, Grimsby is the place to go for fish, Crewe and Rochdale for chips, but for a curry it has to be Bradford City. Valley Parade is situated within a deprived inner city ward, dominated by ethnic minorities and students. It's an elevated area with panoramic views over most of the city As well as curries and a view to thrill lovers of industrial landscapes, there was much real ale to be found. Having munched, supped, and in a couple of strange cases, photographed, we filled the tall but ridiculously narrow new Symphony Stand behind the goal, with the overflow having a bit on the side. The Midland Road Stand at that time was actually little more than an elderly bus shelter. The attendance of 6,600 looked very small on TV.

The scoring pattern was identical to Hartlepool. Just as in the frozen North, Baggies defenders looked angrily at each other as an opponent found ample space to score. This time it was

City's Paul Jewell. Not for the first time, it was SuperBob to the rescue from the penalty spot. Cue predictable chants of *"Oooh Bob Taylor"* and *"You're not singing any more"* from around half the attendance. We might have known that cry would be thrown back at us as the Baggies conceded another silly goal. Ossie chased the game throwing on new boy Hunt. City lost a key defender but was still able to comfortably resist a curious Albion aerial barrage. These weren't Ossie's instructions and said much for the pressure that the players felt. They got lucky. Steve Lilwall's left-wing gallops were making the home side nervous. The Yorkshiremen were struggling and from one Lilwall run and cross, Hunt had a simple tap-in for a debut goal. The relief was immense. This was to be the first of many pairings of Hunt and Taylor on the score sheet, but more immediately, the Baggies had now scored crucial late goals in three straight games. Maybe this side did have some bottle after all?

Whether a draw was satisfactory was much cause for debate. The new evidence of bottle was weighed against the dismal return of two points in 18 on the road. Would it be Play-offs or automatic promotion? More and more supporters were plumping for the former, perhaps as a way of easing their discomfort. This was a painful, agonising promotion chase. After Hunt's debut goal and with the increasingly creaky Garner being substituted again, it made sense to start Hunt in the next home game. The visitors on Grand National Day were themselves play-offs hopefuls - imitation Albion from Sussex. Ardiles' men were rampant, raining in on the visitors' keeper from all sides But Brighton's defence held. Hunt's contribution was lamentable. Somehow in the tension at Bradford, no-one had picked up just how overweight and ring rusty our new arrival really was after two years of reserve team football. Hunt later admitted on his escribbler blog: *"I was very tired after the first half hour and I was off the pace of the game."*

When our name-users took the lead in the second half, all the old fears surfaced once more. After Clive "Flasher" Walker missed a glorious chance for the South-coasters, fear gripped the Hawthorns tightly. Some fans, as ever seeking a scapegoat, were hurling abuse at Hunt while even the moderates wondered why he was still on the pitch. Garner was introduced but to universal booing; it was Mickey Mellon leaving the pitch, not Hunt. Couldn't Ardiles believe the evidence of his own eyes?

'Garns' unsettled B.H.A. with his intelligent runs and passing. The Baggies sought their customary late goal and got it ... in the slightly rotund shape of Andy Hunt. Two minutes later, Hunt was 'right man, right place' again and went on to complete a hat-trick in six minutes. It was accompanied by the sound of jaws dropping around the Hawthorns. Hunt was the first Albion man to score a hat trick on his home debut for 80 years ... and we'd collectively booed him. Whoops. Shades of barracking a Gould home win the previous season.

CB Video interviewed the man of the moment after the game. Hunt looked terribly shy and young, but possessed an agile brain. *"I know I didn't play well. But what's the point of having a blinder if you don't put away your chances?"* (This remark was to haunt him in later years). The following day, Sunday newspapers gave him only 4/10 or 5/10. Understandable, but four goals in one and a bit games was a boost all round. Naturally, Hunt was given the match ball. The whole team signed it with Ossie unable to resist scrawling *"What a buy"* Ardiles had stuck to his principles. Had Hunt been removed from the action, the impact on him, and subsequently the team, may have changed club history.

The victory left the Baggies in 4th place with a genuine feeling that the luck was now going with us. As for Brighton, they'd not lasted the course, rather like the Grand National horses. The big race of the day was famously abandoned after two false starts.

It's routine to make hat-trick men Man of the Match, but Ossie wasn't one for convention. Instead, he singled out another debutant - left back Scott Darton was deputising for Steve Lilwall. *"He's quick, mature, has a quality left foot and wants to be a winner. I thought he was Man of the Match today."*

There was a feel-good factor around the Hawthorns again, as the midweek visitors Swansea were to discover. They were also play-offs contenders, but never recovered from their dreadful defensive error in the first minute. SuperBob said *"ta very much"* and from then on, the Welsh outfit were always vainly chasing the game. They rarely got close. A route one move gave SuperBob yet another goal – his 30th of the season and then Andy Hunt was *"Johnny on the Spot"* with a first-class chip from thirty yards. 3-0 was a fair reflection of a comfortable evening. In truth, the Kettering-born newbie wasn't contributing much ... other than scoring in every game!

After six matches unbeaten, and with a new-found self-belief, travelling to painfully struggling Chester City seemed an ideal opportunity to grab an elusive away win. So it transpired, in what turned out to be one of my most enjoyable away trips ever.

We'd recently endured Port Vale, Hartlepool, Bradford etc so this ancient Roman city with its attendant history and facilities for visitors was simply delightful. Couple this with classic beer garden weather, a new ground, good pubs and it was little wonder that everyone was in good spirits.

My group found Telfords Warehouse, a delightful real ale student boozer on the side of a canal, within walking distance of the ground (just). Supping quality ale on a warm day, overlooking narrowboats ... how often does that happen before any away game? It got better, as one of our gang, Mike Jarvis, hit the jackpot on a fruit machine, leading to free drinks all round.

The Deva stadium was similar to Walsall's original Bescot design, but without the ridiculous pillars. The Deva was all-covered and without fencing. We simply took the place over, filling two and a half sides of the ground, while Chester's 1,000 supporters didn't fill the rest.

All these factors conspired for a carnival atmosphere, but to maintain it required the cornerstone of all the best away matches – an away win. Surely bottom of the table Chester couldn't cope with Albion's twin goal machines? Of course not. Only ten minutes had passed when "*Andy-Hunt-Hunt-Hunt*" slid in his 6th goal in 4 matches. Any sympathy for the hapless Cheshire team was dissipated by their intimidatory tactics – led from the back by their fearsome player-manager, Graham Barrow. "*He kicks anything that moves*" moaned one of his Albion victims later.

Paul Raven dodged the flying bodies to score a second. Chester's Rimmer did manage a neat overhead kick to pull

one back, and Albion briefly wobbled until Donovan's volley wrapped up the game. The end of the match was no more than an exhibition of our attack against their defence as three points were gloriously celebrated. The win raised our total to 72 points – one more than the total for the whole of 1991/92. After much mutual celebration inside the Deva between team and players, the 3,000-strong Baggie army left the ground to Boing excitedly along the solitary exit road. As supporter Mark Wood pointed out *"It was a nice feeling to walk away from the ground with Baggie folk laughing and smiling; if only it could be like this all the time."* But this wasn't quite a paradise trip. The mood of the tramping hordes darkened when various radios announced that Bolton and Vale had won. All that effort, all that excitement, but the gap was still 4 points and now only 6 games left.

The first of those was on Easter Monday with a derby against Plymouth Argyle – albeit a derby for the Green Meanies rather than WBA. Just two days earlier, they'd been thrashed 3-0 at home by Exeter City. Manager Peter Shilton was spitting feathers, but Albion supporters weren't worried. Argyle was only in mid-table after all. Nine minutes gone and SuperBob scored. We were on the way to a seventh straight home win. Except that we weren't. By half time, the wound-up Argyle team were 2-1 ahead and just after the break scored again. The luck was with the visitors, as all their shots hit our net from any distance while Taylor and Hamilton were hitting woodwork rather than net. Aided by some ropey 'keeping by Tony Lange, Argyle eventually won 5-2. It was a simply horrible afternoon. *"What a load of rubbish"* was chanted after the fifth goal was conceded – the 51st League goal in our net thus far. There were far stronger words used at the end, as by common consent, the automatic promotion dream had died. Even the music charts seemed to mock us. At No. 1 was REM's *"Everybody hurts.."* We did.

The few hundred Argyle followers couldn't believe what they were seeing – both on the pitch and around them. A half time celebratory conga was cut short by Albion stewards threatening mass ejection, while the editor of the Plymouth fanzine received the same threat for *"moving around too much."*

The defeat fallout was predictable. Engaging mouth only, Trevor Summers threatened to fine both manager and players. Ossie cancelled the players' day off and had to defend the result to the press. Just a year after Gould had to defend his long ball football, Ardiles was justifying his fluent attacking style. Perhaps the club's problem wasn't about managers, or playing style, but the players.

Many years later Darren Bradley, in conversation with the Albion News said: *"We had got to a point where we thought we were unbeatable. We needed a kick up the backside and Argyle gave it to us. It was a bizarre game but it did us a lot of good."* Such observations can only safely be made in hindsight. There was a frustrated rawness among the Baggie faithful for the rest of the Easter week.

Both players and fans needed a quick pick-up so it was fortunate that the next opponents were more strugglers – Mansfield Town at Field Mill. The East Midlands' town had much of the appeal of Chester (architecture apart!) and offered the added bonus of not being all-ticket.

The Lord Byron is a big pub near the ground. At 12.15 it was quiet and, then somehow within minutes, it was instantly full. It was an extraordinary experience, and I'd swear to this day that Albion supporters were piling in through the windows, as well as the doors.

Being only our second season at this level, we were collectively unaware that Mansfield Town's Unique Selling Point is the unpleasantness of their stewarding, a reputation that they've sturdily maintained since. On selling duty by the official car park entrance, I observed a classic jobsworth in action. Later research indicated that both Frank Worthington and Archie Gemmill had previously been refused admission because *"you're not on my list."* Worthington determinedly argued his corner, but jobsworth held firm. He directed them both to the car park of the Kentucky Fried Chicken where the shop closed during the game and the vehicles duly clamped. Such actions do untold damage on footballers' grapevines. That afternoon, the car park was supposedly full one hour before kick-off. An Albion dignitary in a BMW rolled up and predictably wasn't *"on the list."* The driver remained in the middle of the road for a while before moved on by a WPC. Within minutes, he was back again. Before the attendant could refuse, the driver held out his mobile phone. *"I've got your Chairman on the line. Would you like to have a word?"* The BMW and its driver were speedily admitted. I couldn't help grinning.

Many nervous Albionites entered the ground early. The 600 seats in their impressive main stand (a stripped-down version of Highbury's West Stand) and the 2,600 open unfenced terrace places were quickly filled, with more supporters queuing. Fortunately the Stags opened up part of their side terrace, normally left empty. By kick-off, there were 3,700 Baggie supporters effectively taking up half the ground and outnumbering the home following. *"We are Albion"* loses much on open terracing, but there was little in the way of riposte from Mansfield's own.

The home side may have a game plan but it didn't include conceding after just 31 seconds, Andy Hunt notching his 7th goal in 6 matches. Albion fan Piercey in the Mansfield goal had no chance. The Stags did have a go at our defence and that in turn allowed Ardiles' men to pass the ball around. Six minutes before the interval, Bob Taylor eluded his marker for his 32nd goal and the game was won.

The second half featured a compelling argument against all-seater stadia. Regular Albionite Steve Brooks has a distressing reputation for public flatulence. This match became his most infamous half hour. His Vesuvius-like odours caused great distress for dozens of seated supporters at almost five minute intervals. Having a seat in a sold out stand meant there was no escaping the nostril assault.

Fortunately the on-field action offered distraction. Like Chester, Mansfield couldn't handle Ossie and his diamond. In fact, they completely lost their shape. Defender Chris With (whose brother was a werewolf) was sent off and substitute Carl Heggs added a third for the biggest away win of the season. It could easily have more – Town keeper Pearcey made save after save during the closing minutes. Overall, the mood and belief was buoyant again. This was the Ardiles style in action once more.

Elsewhere, Bolton were beaten but Vale won again so the now third placed Baggies were still 4 points shy of their target. In reality, the Black Country side had been chasing in vain for 15 games, so most were resigned to the unknown Play-Off territory. Indeed, the prospect of actually getting to the twin towers was increasingly beguiling. Wembley was our Camelot, a near-mythical paradise that other football clubs visited. Nearly a quarter of a century had elapsed since the League Cup final visit in 1970. It was a source of constant frustration. The introduction of Play-Off Finals at the twin towers vastly broadened the number of visitors, but the tickets never had our name on them. Older supporters lamented about lost Semi Finals in 1978 and 1982 which derailed our march at the last hurdle. *"Wem-ber-lee it's a place in London that we never get to see."*

But were even the Play-Offs guaranteed? With 75 points already banked and four games remaining, outsiders considered it a done deal but regulars on the Brummie Road weren't so sure. This is Albion, infamous for losing big games. Thus a midweek trip to Reading, yet another play-off hopeful, took on a new dimension. The Berkshire club had won their previous eight home games and really fancied their chances against an Albion side only good enough to beat relegation candidates on the road. The match felt significant – could Ardiles' men stand up and be counted? Yes they could. There was a new determination about the team and a rarely seen aggression, confirmed by a flurry of bookings. Inevitably, SuperBob scored. Inevitably so did Reading, and after that, the two sides slugged it out determinedly but without further score. The draw was well received from the away terrace. We'd had to contend with a noisy Elm Park mob who really believed their team would win but then went curiously AWOL before the end. More importantly, the Baggies had scrapped for a decent result against decent opposition – heartening stuff indeed for the play-offs.

The 3 remaining League games against strugglers Wigan and Hull, plus mid-table Rotherham, sat in a kind of twilight zone. Positive results did matter in the sense of needing to maintain momentum but the burning imperative of "*must win*" was absent. Wembley was on our minds. Not in an arrogant sense (although others would disagree) more in desperation. The need was so palpable that the pitfalls of the Semi Final were mentally pushed aside.

Wigan Athletic were the first of the trio in the penultimate regular League home game. The visitors actually scored first. Their massed ranks of 40 supporters celebrated in the Smerrick. *"That's just going to make our lot mad"* observed the Bloke Behind Me and he was spot on. How different attitudes can be on and off the pitch, when the pressure is eased. Albion were like a tugged-tail tiger. SuperBob scored the equaliser and a blitz of attacking football followed. Mellon, Donovan, Raven and SuperBob all added to the score and Wigan were lucky to get away with just five. Kevin Donovan's third goal was the pick when he bamboozled three defenders and then found the top corner. By then, Wigan knew they were beaten, on their way to a fifth straight defeat and relegation.

Purple-season Bob Taylor remarkably had 35 goals to his name, a total which equalled the best-ever by Ronnie Allen and Jeff Astle (albeit in more matches and against poorer opposition). He'd achieved this total despite much hostile treatment from opponents, and a motley selection of partners. But Albion supporters wanted more. There was still WG Richardson's all-time total of 40 goals to aim for. Despite his goalscoring credentials, the main man was so down to earth. He enjoyed a pint with pretty much anyone, and remained modest. According to his new "bud" Andy Hunt, he was also eccentric *"His team mates all agree that he's got a screw loose. Some of his antics are absolutely hilarious."* There was something about Albion forwards. If Bob Taylor was eccentric; what did that make Carl Heggs? Famously, he'd been persuaded by his team mates to take his driving test in his slippers *"because that's what everyone does..."*

A midweek public PR meeting at West Brom Baths provided diversion from the narrow focus of crucial points-chasing. The free get-together, hosted by Tony Butler, provided an opportunity to ask questions of club directors and consider a wider perspective. The big issue was the Hawthorns becoming all-seater, with director Clive Stapleton trying to sell a plan he didn't fully believe in himself. He pointed out fairly that the football club had limited funds, wanted to live within their means, and thus were limited in what they could afford. As Clive said: *"in my opinion it would be folly on behalf of WBA to build a 40,000 stadium when our maximum average gates would be between 22,000 and 25,000, even in the Premier League."*

Hindsight shows the wisdom of his words but the mass audience that night weren't having any, pointing out that over 15,000 were attending Third Division matches, and claiming *"lack of ambition"*. Clive stuck to his viewpoint, but admitted the capacity did sound "too small."

Supporter after supporter made points, all of which included *"when we get into the Premier League..."* Of course we wanted to believe that, even needed to believe it. After many months of doubt, we were buying into Ossie's dream. Such discussions were both naive and a tad arrogant for a hard-up club yet to escape the third tier, never mind discovering the reality of promotion from the Division above.

In the short term, there were still two League games remaining, including a beachware party in Rotherham. One might imagine that the locals would be grateful to anyone introducing colour into their grim surroundings. There are few football grounds in less appealing areas. Shuttered buildings, closed factories and an enormous scrapyard (owned by club owner Booth) dominated. Far from being grateful, United and the South Yorkshire Police competed for the role of biggest party pooper.

The Police had the first go by refusing to increase our allocation beyond 4,500, even though Rotherham only had 3,500 of their own fans in a 13,000 capacity ground. Ultimately, some ticketless Black Country folk did obtain tickets for the home end. Stoke City fans did the same during an earlier match and violence broke out after City scored. It could so easily have been avoided.

Nearly all the local pubs were closed. Only the ironically-named Travellers Rest, which simply couldn't cope with the weight of bodies, was open. The pub didn't really try too hard to cope. Predictably, many supporters obtained cans and bottles from a local off-licence which, equally predictably, the Police later removed from them.

In what was the peak era for the end-of-season theme, the participation level was spectacular. There were shorts of all colours that defied description. Blue wigs. Pink wigs. White wigs. Balloons, beach balls, plastic bucket and spades. Numerous inflatables too. I had the opportunity to inspect at close range a battery of hammers as they descended on my head. *"Is this all organised?"* exclaimed Brian, co-editor of Rotherham fanzine Mi Whippets Dead. *"We couldn't do anything like that."* For the third away game in a row, our support outnumbered the home following and although it's almost embarrassing to admit this, we strutted like kings in those small towns. *"We are Albion"*.

Our following crammed onto a large covered terrace, and a low, open, fenced seated area on the touchline. The family stand next door was virtually deserted. The brilliant vocal support that afternoon will never quite be forgotten. In what was a pure celebration of being a Baggie, our whole repertoire was aired, including *"The Lord's My Shepherd"* and there was so much optimistic noise about a Wembley trip. The players couldn't fail to be inspired as Darren Bradley confirmed: *"It was amazing to watch from the pitch and it must be great to stand among those involved."*

Rotherham boasted aerial dominance and a surprising amount of brute force for an end of season match with three bookings in the first half. Bob Taylor was wildly hacked by Law, who only received the yellow card. Concerned about the health of his No 1 striker, Ossie protested long and loudly. Good old South Yorkshire Police just had to stick their nose in and "encourage" him to take his seat.

Naturally Law was barracked every time he got close to the ball. He smirked and rubbed his thigh, then pretended to cry after the predictable reaction from the away hordes. He no doubt saw the incident as just end of season banter, but that wasn't our perception ... and where was Inspector Knacker then? A coin was thrown and the situation could easily have become more serious. As it happened, United's former Albion man Varadi was sent off after disputing a disallowed goal. After that the Rotherham mob had to concentrate on keeping a clean sheet.

They didn't succeed. Paul Raven scored from a corner with two minutes left. Most of our team hung on the dividing fence to celebrate with the bouncing beachwear crew. It meant nothing to the wider world that were focussing on Brian Clough's retirement that afternoon, but for 4,500 people penned up next to a South Yorkshire scrap yard, it meant so much. The Police responded by lining up a row of officers and

dogs in front of our seated supporters. This compelled everyone to stand and created much unnecessary tension. It also obscured SuperBob clinching the match in injury time. Such was the good humour, everyone was able to concentrate on the positives, and created such a good vibe that celebrations continued late in the night. (Many years later, South Yorkshire Police did their best to spoil another promotion celebration at Doncaster.) But the following morning, the all-embracing monster of the Play-Off Semi-Finals felt very close.

The following evening saw Player of the Year night at a sold out Kings nightclub in Great Barr. The real highlight was the unfettered association between supporters and the players and the mutual respect this engendered. Supporters, and probably some players too (though they wouldn't admit to it in public) were feeling the pressure of the most intense promotion campaign since 1976. Various team members were told half-seriously to *"mind those steps"* or *"be careful with that piece of chicken".*

For the final regular League home match, the programme included a Wembley voucher – just in case. For the same reason, over 20,000 people turned up. It led to rather unseemly squabbles for programmes, with fans in the Brummie queuing for 30 minutes to buy from the beleaguered two sellers. Only 4,000 extra copies were printed, and as stocks ran down, tempers frayed. In the end, Albion withdrew them from sale which spared the sellers, but did nothing for their public relations. Hull City turned up only in body and the Baggies strolled to their 17th home win. Almost inevitably, SuperBob and Andy Hunt both found the net as the stars in stripes won 3-1.

Long before kick-off, WBA were guaranteed to finish fourth and thus had the reassurance of a home second leg on Wednesday May 19. All six Play-Off Second Legs were scheduled for that night in the days before Sky took an interest. Yet Albion's opponents were not decided until the last minute of the last game. A 89th minute Huddersfield winner against Stockport dropped County to sixth spot leaving Swansea in fifth to play the Baggies. Our track record against the white shirted Welshmen was far stronger and we needed all the positive omens we could get.

The final table revealed just how unusually strong the top four sides really were. Albion's 85 points was only enough for 4th spot but 12 months earlier, would have made them Champions. Albion had scored in every League game in 1993 and amassed over 100 goals in all competitions (the second highest scorers in the country). WBA had lost only once in the last 13 games, yet that wasn't consistent enough to match Bolton who took the second automatic spot behind Stoke City. Port Vale amassed 89 points and missed promotion by a single point. They'd accused their neighbours Stoke of lying down and dying in a key end of season game against Bolton. Any result, other than a Wanderers win, would have seen Vale promoted instead, they lamented. Naturally the lardy men expect any other result.

Both the Albion team and their supporters alike were naive about what was needed to win the play-offs. No supporters (and few of the players) had any previous experience. The end of season promotion decider was still a relatively new concept. The Wembley Finals only started in 1990. We'd had two-legged matches before but few, if any, with such pressure since the 1982 League Cup Semi and none with such a prize or overwhelming tension.

In an unwelcome distraction just two days before the Semi-Final, the Spurs Board sacked Chief Executive Terry Venables on the casting vote of Alan Sugar. That evening, a judge temporarily quashed the sacking although it would only delay the inevitable parting. Venables was popular, so Sugar was vilified for his actions. The drama seemed a world away from our own concerns, although there were a few jokes about our own manager replacing him.

A goodly proportion of the 2,000+ with tickets for the Vetch (plus the 3,000 watching on a big screen in the NIA) went in search of Dutch courage in Swansea. The nearest boozer, the Glamorgan, was under siege from midday. All visitors were welcome, explained mine host genially. *"I never have problems with away supporters, just home ones."* Among the early arrivals were a small group of Bristol City supporters, there to back Bob Taylor. They were an invaluable source of fascinating SuperBob tales, such as the time he signed autographs while on a stretcher.

The news that the Glamorgan was running out of alcohol only intensified the pressure. A supply of canned lager appeared from somewhere, but didn't last long, leaving just soft drinks. There was a perverse pride in drinking a pub dry but equally frustration for those who couldn't watch Albion sober. In desperation, supermarket warm beer just had to do.

The rest of Swansea was anything but dry with teeming rain.

This was a hindrance both for Ossie's men, who found

accurate passing difficult and the half of the away contingent that couldn't force access under the semi roofed enclosure. A few who'd sheltered in the toilet until kick-off were easily recognisable by the cobwebs on their heads and their sodden shoes and socks. Swans toilets were always notorious but on this day, they overflowed to ankle height.

The day went downhill rapidly. Swansea were quicker to the ball and physically stronger and however much we tried to back our team, Albion remained second best. I'd wanted the game to start so badly ... and when it did start,I wanted it over. Early in the second half, Swansea full back Des Lyttle set up his big striker McFarlane perfectly in the penalty box. His strength took him past a lunging challenge from Raven and suddenly the Swans were a goal up. There was worse, far worse, to follow when Andy Legg outpaced Raven and crossed for Martin Hayes to easily beat Lange. Two goals down, and feeling very very wet, the mood in the away end was grim. Our dream was dying in the South-West Wales mud. To our left, our right and above us, there were Welshmen in song. Given the 14,000 attendance was almost treble their 5,000 average gate, probably many were miming. The noise couldn't quite block out the laments from soggy and cobwebbed Black Country heads - where were our team's kahunas?

There was an answer ... from an unexpected source. The unlikely form of central defender Daryl Burgess squelched determinedly into the opposition box, having flicked the ball over a defender. Despite the certain knowledge he'd get whacked, Daryl went for the kill. He lobbed the ball over the onrushing keeper. It struck the bar and hit the knees of McFarlane who could do nothing to stop it crossing the line. While Albion supporters everywhere roared their relief, Daryl slumped to the turf in pain. His willingness to take a big hit for the team had cost him, so much so that his season was over.

To their credit, his team mates were more concerned about "Burge" than celebrating the goal.

According to Ian Hamilton: *"to get that goal back was really important. That changed the whole feel of everything."* Back in the day away goals counted double, so the sacrifice of one man made Wembley reachable. With a substitute on to replace the stricken Burgess, Albion collectively gritted their teeth and kept the Swans at bay for the remaining 15 minutes. I was simply numb in the away end. Couldn't feel tension, excitement, nerves .. just nerves. This was just the starter. The main course was still to follow.

Frustrated locals took out their frustration on our cars, minibuses, coaches and anyone who wasn't Welsh was fair game. Teeming rain, a smashed windscreen and a long trip home is a horrible combination.

Swansea manager Frank Burrows knew his best chance of success had slipped away. He was up against a side with five players with 8 or more goals to their name, 17 home League wins and supporters about to give Welsh people singing lessons. They'd be no welcome in Sandwell Valley.

Has any Albion game before or since been so eagerly anticipated and feared at the same time? Glynis Wright's memories of that night were probably typical. *"I woke up tense that morning and completed the daytime work duties in a dream. All I could think of was the game that night. Incredible, the number of Seal and Wulf colleagues who popped into my office to wish me luck. It was distinctly disturbing behaviour, most unlike them. Was this a trap?*

Four o'clock and one quick change later, I was heading for the Woodman. I arrived to find the place pretty crowded already with Albionites alcoholically endeavouring to anaesthetise their pre-match nerves. Mine were in a pretty shaky state already: only one thing to do, join them! Halfway through my second double, I took stock of my surroundings. You could almost smell the fear in that small lounge despite lusty cries of "Wember-lee". They always let you down (the fanzine motto) we reminded ourselves ad nauseum. Ossie's team and 20,000+ crowds were unhappy bedfellows. The tension got to me and it was a relief to leave the pub. No amount of alcohol would take the edge off that burden. It was also such a relief to see two magpies strutting on the lawn on the opposite side of the Brummie Road. Call me superstitious if you like, but from then on, I had no doubt this would be our year."

Defeat in this win-or-else encounter didn't bear thinking about. A third season in the third, finances even more stretched, better players seeking their fortune elsewhere. Ardiles was clear *"Losing will cost Albion their best players."* Or, as author Richard Brentnall had it, *"the second leg presented a scenario that all too often in the past resulted in an Albion nightmare of crushing disappointment."*

Your first anything is special. First girl or boyfriend, losing your virginity, first job, first car – you never forget. At the age of 33, I'd never seen my team play at Wembley and like so many Wembley virgins, I would scream, sing, shout, beg whatever it took to boost my team towards those twin towers with what supporter Benjamin Watts aptly described as "frenzied desperation." Almost all of a near sell-out Hawthorns (Swansea had some returns), felt the same way. The Brummie set the example with an unearthly volume of sound, closely followed by the rest of the stadium.

The Albion side matched the mood perfectly, and joyfully took an aggregate lead after just seven minutes. SuperBob found space for young Andy Hunt to beat Freestone, and the roar of triumph was probably audible in West Brom town centre. Years later, SuperBob admitted to the club programme: *"I just went ballistic after the goal, like a banshee, a man possessed and I was. I was that wound up because we needed to win, and everybody else was like that."*

Somehow this was bettered when Ian Hamilton implausibly scored the second goal from a ridiculous angle *"My best moment personally"* admitted the midfielder later. There will never be a goal celebration to equal this - seemingly all 5,000 inhabitants in the Brummie Road boinging in harmony. The concrete structure flexed under the strain – as much as three inches with each Boing - according to director Clive Stapleton. The staff in the refreshment hut underneath vainly tried to block the cascade of items leaping off their shelves. *"Wem-ber-lee..."*

Albion were on top. They were missing chances, but comfortable, albeit deafened. Some players claimed even the pitch was shaking. The Swansea men couldn't communicate while manager Burrows couldn't get information out, even with a megaphone.

The game threatened to turn when Mickey Mellon was sent off in the second half. This was painful enough, but then defender Paul Raven had to take time out for a head wound. The nine remaining players formed a thin defensive cordon as best they could. *"When the chips are down, you play on adrenalin and when the crowd is completely behind you, the adrenalin is really pumping"* explained Kevin Donovan but would that be enough? Bob Taylor, temporarily in midfield, wasn't the only star in stripes *"wondering whether we can hang on."* The vocal support took on a new ragged, desperate edge.

Trainer Danny Thomas had never had so much pressure to treat an injury quickly. Ossie was under even more pressure from eye-bulging incandescent supporters all round to make an immediate substitution, but both hung tough. Had the Welshman's McFarlane put away either of the two headed chances during that period, our history may have been very different.

But the Gods were on our side. Our bandaged defender returned to the pitch. Better still, Swansea substitute Colin

West was so desperate to make a mark that he did so on Ian Hamilton, rather than on the game. To massive relief and cheers, he was sent off. Back on level terms numerically, Albion just had to see out the remaining minutes in a rising cauldron of nervous noise. Kevin Donovan again: *"towards the end, the noise was deafening. We couldn't speak to each other because you just couldn't hear anything over the crowd."* Triumphant chants about Wembley grew louder and louder as we dared to believe. Wembley, Wembley, always Wembley – an end in itself, rather than a means to an end.

Club stewards were diverted from their duties to form a defensive line around the pitch, among them Dave Woodhall: *"I swear I could feel vibrations through the pitch because of the boinging."*

With minutes remaining, Darren Bradley broke clear of all the Swansea defence with a perfect chance to end the finger-chewing tension. He seemed to run in slow motion before shooting at Freestone tamely. It was the last of several glorious opportunities wasted, but Albion had done enough. The end of the game was seen rather than heard. Wembley. Such eight letters but it meant so much for so many.

Amid the inevitable pitch invasion, Steve Lilwall was seen to leap into the arms of any supporters. His team mates gave their shirts and other items to the bouncing hordes. As Andy Hunt later remembered on his blog *"I made it back to the dressing room with just my boots and underwear on. Some lucky fan got a pair of stinky socks for their trouble."* Bob Taylor was chaired all the way to the Brummie Road End, where he needed the help of a forceful five man Police escort to get back to the dressing room. The plods probably wondered why they bothered because two minutes later, Bob ran out to the Brummie once more with a shirt in his hand and was mobbed for a second time. As Craig Shakespeare said, it was *"wonderful to see so much happiness on so many faces."*

Tears were quietly shed as a lifetime's ambition became real. Not one usually given to emotion, historian Steve Carr recalled *"the feeling of joy at the final whistle still remains the single most ecstatic moment of all my years following the Albion. Tears were shed and I was hugging and being hugged by everybody and anybody stood in my vicinity, Even now, reading about this game or watching action from it on DVD causes me to start welling up again."*

No one wanted to leave, and thus the players returned for a lap of honour in their remaining clothing, but not before the repeated playing of the Liquidator. Ardiles joined the players, who managed to get almost all the way around the pitch without being mobbed.

It was already late, but many were too high to go home and needed to share their excitement. Staff at the Woodman (and other local pubs) couldn't pull pints fast enough. From the beer garden behind the pub, Swansea coaches quietly left, seemingly without even any engine noise. It was a poignant moment and although a few noisy Baggies mocked, others remained as quiet as the coaches, thinking they'd been on that silent vehicle too often. Defeat would cost Swansea. Their better players such as Des Lyttle would leave for bigger clubs and within three years, they were relegated to the basement Division. Over a decade and a half would elapse before they could challenge for promotion to the second tier.

In the light of a ground bulging at the seams for this unique encounter, Trevor Summers was pressed about the future size of the Hawthorns. *"I am a prat"* he exclaimed as his brain tried vainly to catch up with his mouth. *"We have to find another 6,000 seats from somewhere."* Cue the rest of the Board bellowing *"Nooooo"* with heads in their hands, anticipating another awkward meeting with the bank manager.

The Vale fanzine "Seth Bottomley" nominated Trevor Summers for a "Moaning Git of the Year" award. After making various allegations, the editorial added *"What an irritating face. When in full flow during his moaning extravaganzas on Central TV or BBC Midlands, doesn't that face just plead to be hit repeatedly with a garden rake?"* Whilst OTT, there were times when most Baggies did wish he'd simply keep quiet.

The sale of Wembley tickets were shockingly inefficient, and made considerably worse by single-minded supporters. The football club declared they would use a sales technique made famous in World War 2 – a queue. Doesn't matter where you live or what hours you might work, the tickets would be on sale via three turnstiles on Saturday morning. No credit cards, no telephone bookings, no postal applications, thank you very much. Oh and bring your own refreshments and make sure you go to the toilet before you leave the house. We were supposed to be grateful that the Junior Baggies allocation, originally a parental-stress-inducing one ticket per membership, had been revised upwards. But it was now an over-generous three, thus giving kids who paid a few quid for their membership, having a larger allocation than season ticket holder (two per book).

The refugee-like column started to form the previous night and simply grew and grew. With no assistance from the club, supporters made their own arrangements, liberating tarpaulins and wood from a building site to provide heat and cover. With a 27 hour wait ahead, they felt fully justified.

By opening time, the line snaked round and round the Rainbow Stand car park. The front group had a map of Wembley seating with them and had picked out exactly the tickets they wanted next to the Royal Box. In their eyes, they were first in the queue and should have first pick. The ticket office staff knew they weren't available, because they'd already been pre-allocated. The supporters repeated their arguments and added they wouldn't budge until they got their way. Result - a two hour impasse, during which the waiting queue now stretched for over a mile. Moods darkened.

I got my tickets after a four hour wait. Although I didn't feel that fortunate after such a leg-aching, dehydrating delay, I was comparatively fortunate. As selling didn't start until 11.00am and the length of the queue startled everyone, by late afternoon the club realised their antediluvian selling plan wouldn't work. Their tiny sales team were exhausted serving an increasing fractious line. A decision was needed to stop selling and reconvene on a later day. Naturally, it was badly received.

Young season ticket holder Darren Rampling reluctantly travelled from London to buy a ticket. He vehemently protested that he couldn't come again due to work. He became so upset that he was threatened with arrest. He broke down and cried on the side of the road. His Dad Laurie Rampling was maddened. *"The way I feel at this moment, I will never set foot again in the Hawthorns."* Had not common sense prevailed and an arrangement made later for young Darren, Laurie's photographic skills may have gone elsewhere.

Albion extended their days of sale but it was obvious that demand was going to exceed their supply, even with a further batch from a surprised Wembley. Our following ultimately totalled 42,000, a record support for a single club in the third tier play-offs (a figure which held until Man City's masses in 1999). . Meanwhile 45 miles up the road, Port Vale had tens of thousands of tickets and no buyers, yet they stubbornly refused to release any more to their opposition.

The Potteries outfit had sold 11,000 tickets against their average home attendance of 8,000. Even some of these were bought by Potteries-based Albion supporters persuaded to make several visits to do favours for desperate exiles. It was straight-in, straight out each time with no questions asked. Mind, they did speak "Stokie." Vale's excuse was that their supporters had two Wembley trips in eight days and couldn't afford both. Port Vale beat Stockport in the Autoglass (Football League) Trophy and judging by the 27,000 behind Vale that afternoon, their supporters considered the Autoglass to be more important.

Increasingly frantic ticket hunters from the Black Country pointed out Vale followers had had over a hundred years to save up for Wembley trips. Hindsight shows that five years later, Grimsby Town, a smaller club further away from London, found 30,000 supporters to back their Autoglass triumph at Wembley and four weeks later, took the same number to the same venue for a Play Off Final.

At some point before the Final, Ardiles was discreetly sounded out by Tottenham. Spurs joint managers Ray Clemence and Doug Livermore had been obliged to follow Venables through the exit doors. Feeling heavy heat from making unpopular decisions, Alan Sugar needed a supporter-appeasing new manager. Ardiles was torn, but had promised himself back in 1988 when he left White Hart Lane that he would return, given the chance. He told the Spur fanzine months later *"If*

somebody had come to me before, I would have said yes.
Spurs is my second home in England." Hints in tabloid
newspapers suggested the sounding-out or even talks about
talks, may have pre-dated the Baggies beating Swansea.
A visit to England's most iconic stadium is high stakes for
every supporter but few more so than Newcastle, Staffs-based
Baggie Martin Lewis. He worked at Wedgwood's, where, not
surprisingly, he was the sole representative of Vale's
opponents. He was the handkerchief nestling between two
metaphorical tug-of-war teams. There were Stoke supporters
insisting *"you'd better not lose to that lot"* while Valeites were
telling him that's exactly what Albion would be doing.
With such personal high stakes, he arrived at the Wright
household a full hour early on the big day, unable to sleep. But
as the Wright household were also equally sleepless in
Smethwick, and fully alert, this was no hardship. We were all
behaving like small children about to embark on a great
adventure.

T
he adventure really started with the first view of Wembley's

superstructure. It was final confirmation that West Bromwich Albion really were in town. There were looks of wonderment on the faces of young supporters .. and many older ones too. Our coach resembled a school trip seeing the sea for the first time. In his eloquent escriber blog, Andy Hunt also got that Wembley feeling. *"I had been to Wembley before as a spectator, but arriving at the stadium in the coach as one of the players was, well, surreal. Souvenir stalls, fans everywhere, hotdog stalls, the vibrant colours of the team flags all around us, was just breathtaking. "*

The Albion coach was treated like a royal carriage, with an enormous security presence surrounding it like an honour guard. Curiously, all the security were wearing WBA shirts. At a slow walking speed, the coach edged forward before entering the Wembley gates. In contrast, the Vale coach had no support, and no welcome. Just lots of torment from Albionites asking *"Who are you?"*

For so many including most of the Albion team, it was their first visit to the twin towers. Andy Hunt again: *"I didn't really know what to expect once inside Wembley. Gold baths, ivory*

bath taps, opulence everywhere. *Sounds stupid, but you just don't know what to expect when you enter the stadium. Actually, the changing rooms and surrounding area were spacious but not very much different to other stadiums."*

First-time supporters were discovering how dilapidated the place really was, an old whore of a stadium trading on its past glories. The toilets were primitive. The outrageously priced catering points were unable to cope with demand. Many of the so-called seats were backless stools. The sightlines were poor and the high fencing was cage-like. The stairs felt endless. My group had luckily acquired front row seats on the top deck. Other than a slightly alarming feeling of vertigo, most everything else was first-rate. Like everyone else, we were in our seats ridiculously early. The scenes resembled a cross between a Nuremberg rally and the Circus Maximus in one half of the stadium. The other end was primarily empty seats. Nerves were taking hold. Glynis Wright: *"I had an overwhelming feeling of cold –or pre-match nerves."* We could only guess how the team were feeling.

Andy Hunt: *"It was only when you entered the pitch that the heart started to jump a beat. Wembley looks huge from the inside. We walked the field in our terrible Wembley suits. Many of the players had got their trousers mixed up, so the trousers were an inch too long or an inch too short."*

As the big kick–off approached, Bob Taylor revealed in conversation with Chris Lepkowski: *"it wasn't until we walked out for the game that it hit us. Back then, they had a canvas tunnel which stretched out pretty much across the greyhound track, right up to the goal and all we could see in front of us were empty seats - not realising that's where Port Vale fans were supposed to be sitting. If you watch a video of the game now you can see all the players suddenly turning round when they hear the noise behind them from the 42,000 Albion fans. It was incredible and the noise was deafening."*

In such overwhelming winner-takes-it-all circumstances, every pass became significant. Any attack from either side becomes stressful. After 45 minutes of such tension but no goals, it was debatable who were the better side, but there was little doubt that the Baggies were getting their passing game together just before half-time. There was much ire focused on Kevin Donovan for not converting his chances.

When Peter Swan infamously brought Bob Taylor down on the edge of the box, referee Milford spotted the professional foul and sent the defender off. In his biography, the Vale man admitted "*I had to run the gauntlet of the West Brom fans as I made my way to the dressing room. What really hurt was the sound of some fans laughing at me. It seemed I was just a joke to them.*"

Vale being reduced to ten men was Albion's big chance and they took it.

Andy Hunt: "*Twisting like an eel, I directed a soft header into the corner of the net. WOW. Scoring at Wembley. Off I ran to the corner flag to dance my little jig, and celebrate like crazy with the team. My God. You have never had adrenaline pumping like this unless you've hit a home run or sky dived from an aeroplane. The hard part was "coming down" again to cool my head and carry on the game.*" All around him, Albion supporters screamed, shouted, hugged and cried. Potteries-based Martin Lewis completely lost himself in joy, and would had fallen from the top deck if other hands hadn't grabbed him.

Hunt's goal probably would have secured promotion by itself. But we wanted more, needed more and seven minutes from time, Nicky Reid chose the best possible moment for his only Albion goal. As we blissfully boinged, we knew this time Albion really weren't going to let us down. Just to prove it, Donovan pinched the ball off Bob Taylor as he was about to pull the trigger himself, and scored. Oh joy joy joy. 3-0 remained the biggest margin of victory in the third level Play-offs until 2015.

After endless full-blooded choruses of *"We are Going Up"*, a small Argentinian changed everyone's tune. *"**Ossie's** **Barmy** **Army**"* was the new ditty, with a slightly greater emphasis on his name each time. His body language suggested embarrassment, but at that time we all considered him modest.

And then ... and then all the Cup winning rituals followed. Rituals that we'd all observed other clubs savouring over the last couple of decades. But now, at last, it was our turn. Darren Bradley lifted the strange looking trophy with a manic grin followed by the compulsory lap of honour.

Bob Taylor felt embarrassed for his former Leeds team mate, and made a point of seeking out Peter Swan's parents to say sorry. He need not have worried, as Swan himself later explained to the Sunday Times:

"I was gutted. On the bus home I sat at the front by myself. I couldn't face my teammates. Then one of the lads put a bottle of champagne in front of me and told me to join them at the back. Two-and-a-half hours later, we were all in good spirits. We had a Madness CD which we played to and from games. We started to overtake the buses carrying the West Brom fans on the motorway and we were all dancing to Madness up and down our bus with black glasses on. We saw the West Brom fans and they looked like they had just got beaten. They must have thought we were crazy. For a party piece, a few bare backsides were waved in their direction as we drove by."

Twelve months later, Port Vale were promoted automatically. Not every Baggie had happy memories of the Big Day. David Valder lives in Brighton but knew there was only one Albion. Despairing of even trying to get tickets with "his own", he applied by post to Port Vale who were content to send him four tickets without question – one for him and three relatives all of whom followed imitation Albion. David deliberately based his group in an isolated corner. Unwisely, he couldn't help celebrating Andy Hunt's goal after which a Vale fan ran down six rows of seats to hit him on the back of the head. David missed the rest of the game receiving medical attention.

The antics of South-Wales based "character" Colin Wood has previously featured in these pages. Sad to relate that Colin overdid the pre-match drinking to such a degree he was ejected from Wembley after a few minutes play for being "*drunk and disorderly*". What a waste.

Days after promotion and a celebratory open-top bus tour richly given colour by Andy Hunt's state of intoxication, Albion's manager was asked about future plans. *"I've got the players in mind. I know exactly what I want – in fact, I've known for quite a while."* It was accepted at the time as a positive statement of intent. But what he really, really wanted didn't become public knowledge for weeks.

Ardiles had a confession to make, but ducked the issue for a while, ultimately making the news even more desirable.

Before flying out to Argentina in mid-June, he'd assured the directors that he wanted to stay despite newspaper stories to the contrary. He was a Gentleman after all. A week later, Spurs had his autograph. Trevor Summers was in bulldog-like mood. "*We are going to war on this.*" There was more. *"If Alan Sugar thinks he can just walk in and take West Bromwich Albion's manager, I'll be down that motorway like an Exocet to blow up his bloody computers."* Sigh. Fellow director Tony Hale was more sagacious. *"I cannot describe how I feel about Ardiles action this week. He told me he was happy to stay and finish the job on Monday. Come Saturday, he'd left to join Spurs."*

Ardiles' protest that "*it was an affair of the heart, Spurs are in my blood*" didn't soften the blow. We were universally distraught with the knife twisted further with the Argentinian's ill-judged TV remark that he'd *"only needed five seconds to make up his mind."* It was a faux pas worthy of Prince Phillip, never mind Trevor Summers. Later when tempers had calmed a little, our ex-manager tried to explain via an interview with the Spur fanzine *"I meant the "five second" quote as a joke. It was on a television interview the day I signed here. There was a lot of tension around, and I decided to try and crack a joke to relax everybody. But it was obviously in very poor taste. The supporters were very good to me. They took me to my hearts so I apologised to them later."*

Author Richard Brentnall was ironically holidaying in Argentina with mates when he spotted a newspaper picture of a grinning Alan Sugar and Ossie Ardiles. *"We spoke of the heroic futility of being an Albion supporter, whereby promise turns into a kick in the balls, and whereby whenever we have someone special he pisses off elsewhere, and whereby we'll nevertheless keep coming for more, despondent or not."*

Keep calm and carry on, in other words. There wasn't much else supporters could do during the isolation of the summer shutdown.   After their high level debate, Richard and his chums then got themselves royally drunk. It was a common reaction.

Trevor Summers wasn't sounding very calm. *'I'm totally devastated. He has let us all down. Fifty thousand Black Country lads had taken him - an Argentinian - to their hearts, and he's let them down.'*   The Albion Board opted for legal action against Ardiles. They considered that although there was no written contract of employment, the fact that he'd been on the payroll for a year and taken a £50,000 bonus for winning promotion meant that a contract existed.

Unfortunately verbal frameworks include no definitive exit policy.

Ardiles: *"The Albion directors got a writ and sent it to me at 7.00am. They had a photographer there (from the Sun) and that was completely and utterly out of order. For some reason they wanted to have maximum publicity. I don't know why, because they don't win any friends by doing these things. It was a kind of vengeance and the action of ungrateful men."* Indeed it was, but those ungrateful men were also maddened by his less than frank approach, and the brutally selfish nature of the professional game. Had he taken the line there was only so much begging, borrowing and calling in favours from old mates that he could do to compensate for Albion's cash shortages, then his exit would have been more charitably received.

WBA's annual accounts made for disturbing reading. Once transfers were taken into account, Albion made a loss of £254,000 in a promotion season, despite income increasing by over 50%. These were worrying figures – if the Baggies couldn't turn in a profit now, when would they ever? Over the year, the directors had resisted supporters' pressure to "spend big" but were cornered into authorising some transfers to give Ardiles a realistic chance of promotion. Despite another excitable quote from Trevor Summers after the Wembley triumph that *"we will spend a million quid on players"* ,the club was cash-strapped and only just legally solvent, thanks to the nominal value of the Halfords Lane stand.

Attitudes have changed greatly in the intervening quarter century. Nowadays, it would be a major surprise if a former World Cup winner **didn't** leave an impoverished Third Division club for a leading Premiership outfit. That's even assuming such a luminary would lower himself to such a level in the first place. But, then, as now, there are clubs on the up and clubs which are impossible to move forward. Ardiles would learn which was which the hard way. *"Choosing Tottenham at the time was a big mistake - something I realised much later in my life"* admitted Ossie to the Birmingham Mail almost two decades later.

More immediately, Albion needed a new man in charge and asked Burkinshaw to take over. The 'Burk' didn't have much of a choice to make. He'd already previously admitted his distaste for the ways Spurs operated and although Ossie wanted to take him along, it was only to fill an unspecified role. He accepted the Albion job, prompting another Summers classic *'The apprentice has gone, but the professional has stayed.'* We would see.

Acknowledgements

Writing about West Bromwich Albion should never be a solo occupation so I'm very grateful for so much encouragement and inspiration from so many supporters. Thus I'm indebted to: Steve Sant, Dean Walton, Terry Wills, Richard Brentnall, Glynis Wright, Neil Reynolds, Martin Lewis, Dean Wood, Steve Brooks, Mark Wood, Richard Ryan, the Bloke(s) behind me, Mark Wilson, Norman Catton, Ian 'Patch' Partridge, Peter Betteridge, Kev Candon, Conrad Chircop, and Norman Bartlam

Amanda Hume, Glynis "Boss" Wright and Steve Carr patiently proofread without many complaints. Any remaining errors are down to me.

The formal reference sources include Grorty Dick fanzine, Last Train to Rolfe Street fanzine, the Sports Argus, The Birmingham Evening Mail, The Albion News and the biographies of Bobby Gould, Ossie Ardiles, Peter Swan and Andy Hunt (electronic)

Photographs from Glynis Wright, Dean Walton and Graham Dring

19137591R00096

Printed in Great Britain
by Amazon